God, Evolution, and Evil's Mystery

Julian Fernandes

God, Evolution, and Evil's Mystery

Julian Fernandes

Abstract

The purpose of this thesis is to offer a defence for the goodness of the God of the Judeo/Christian Scriptures—in the light of [the Triune] God's use of an evolutionary process; a process that has predation, pain and death as an essential core of its potential, *id est*, to give rise to the 'end purposes (*telos*) of God'. The methodological approach taken in this thesis is one in which the shape of the account is determined by Christian doctrine—the scientific contribution being critically appropriated to that doctrinally shaped account.

Under the heading of 'Changes to the traditional/Biblical view of the attributes of God' we consider the implications/alternatives espoused by some philosophical theologians. This section of the thesis explores the alternative views of the 'nature' and 'attributes' of God, id est, the transposition of the God of Scripture with another in the light of the problem of natural evil—that of a creative 'ground of being' that is deemed more acceptable to both science and modern philosophical theology. Further to its research objectives the thesis investigates recent evolutionary defences/theodicies offered by several proponents of both scientific enquiry and theological research and reflection.

The final part of the thesis offers an eight-step argument for the goodness and justice of God in the light of evolution—an argument that has developed out of the author's work regarding God, evolution and the [evidential] problem of evil. A major part of the argument centres on the pre-cosmological existence of angels and the rebellion of those considered 'fallen'.

God, Evolution, and Evil's Mystery

Julian Fernandes

Contents

Part One

God, Evolution, and Evil's Mystery
Julian Fernandes

Part Two

An Eight Step Defence

Step 1. It is good for God to create a world containing beauty, diversity and complexity of creatures.

Step 2. Such a world can only arise via an evolutionary process, which also necessitates suffering and apparent waste.

Step 3. Only such a world is capable of being transformed into the 'new creation', in which there need be no more suffering.

Step 4. But also, there is evidence that angels exist.

Step 5. That Angels may have existed before the creation of this universe

Step 6. That it is a good thing that God gave angels freedom:

    6.1 Free Will, Angels and Sovereignty

Step 7. That angels rebelled and continued to oppose God's will for humans and the rest of creation:

God, Evolution, and Evil's Mystery

Julian Fernandes

God, Evolution, and Evil's Mystery
Julian Fernandes

Part One

1. Introduction

The interest for the subject of this thesis emanates from the conviction that the God of the Judeo/Christian Scriptures (_The creator of all things ex nihilo_) is both Omnipotent and Benevolent; and __this__ in the light of an evolutionary process that is, seemingly, the root cause of suffering—a process that may be described as that through which, "...thousands of animals are being eaten alive; others are running for their lives, whimpering with fear; others are being slowly devoured from within by rasping parasites..." [etc..] (**Dawkins 1996, 132**)

The word benevolence is, as McCabe (**2010, 56**) reports Aquinas as saying, "...used '_secundum analogiam_' (according to analogy)...The inferences in the case of God fail because 'good' is a contextually dependant word." Though it is the case that Aquinas thought that evil was, most often, the absence (privation) of positive outcomes; it can be argued, as we do, that to say that God's benevolence always has to be interpreted as God's having to bring about 'good outcomes for whosoever—whether justified outcomes or not is mistaken; this is not to deny God's right to forgive but God's right to bring about a just state of affairs.

Clearly a theistic view of the creation must attribute some intentionality within the process of natural selection—a process that may be described as 'purpose-driven'. Evolution in this thesis is taken to be the process through which [God], rather than entirely unguided materialistic processes, has brought about the best possible conditions for the development of life and consciousness—the process through which God will bring about His ultimate goal—at the eschatological climax of God's creation.

God, Evolution, and Evil's Mystery

Julian Fernandes

Dennis Lamoureux (**2013**) offers an evolutionary theological perspective that he refers to as 'Evolutionary Creationism': "Evolutionary creation asserts that the Father, Son, and Holy Spirit created the universe and life, including humans, through an ordained, sustained and intelligent design-reflecting evolutionary process." (**42,43**) It is from the perspective of a 'purpose-driven natural process' that the argument in this thesis is developed.

Since the advent of Darwinism—and because of the increasing challenge of Naturalistic Materialism—there is an increasingly urgent need for a fresh approach to the subject of theodicy. As a result of a developing (hostile) narrative the existence of the God of the Bible is in question or simply classified along with 'fairy story' narratives—as being blatantly false. The second reason for the undertaking of this research is because of a personal dissatisfaction with theodicies/defences of:

i)   a traditional genre i.e. 'Fall' defences that offer the actions of the man and woman in the 'Garden of Eden' as ***the sole*** reason for the predation, parasitism and plague experienced by all carbon-based life-forms since the beginning of time—or in this case since the disobedience of the first humans.

ii)   defences that offer naturalistic explanations, philosophical speculation or dialectical reasoning—without major consideration for what Scripture may teach regarding past and future events.

This thesis is concerned with the problem of suffering among sentient creatures of all varieties in the light of evolutionary processes that have been a part of life's

God, Evolution, and Evil's Mystery

Julian Fernandes

progression from its genesis. This is not to say that there were would not have been significant 'effects' initiated by God after the Fall of mankind as Scripture indicates; neither is it to say that fallen angels have not, do not and will not bring about states of affairs that have increased, do increase and will increase the potential of suffering for sentient life-forms. On the contrary, Scripture makes clear that such causes and effects proceeded from both the fall of angels and of mankind. Moreover, it is the case that mankind itself is responsible for an unfathomable amount of suffering—whether through his moral ineptitude or through his abuse/misuse of God given natural resources.

The thesis considers the extent to which this suffering acts as a charge against either the power or the goodness of God. The thesis addresses the problem from a position of belief and commitment to a view of God's character and attributes—as offered by the Scriptures rather from any modern/post-modern notion of the 'person'/character of God. The argument in this thesis offers what may be considered a fresh approach to the problem—an approach which is consistent with the Scriptures or with theistic evolutionary views of God's 'eternal' perspectives—his 'plans and purposes' for the created order.

The approach to this work is of a theological/scientific nature rather than a purely scientific, philosophical approach. The reasons for taking the theological/scientific approach are due, in particular, to the nature of the 'charge' against God—not any 'god' but, specifically, the God of the Bible—that biological evolutionary processes cannot be harmonized with any notion of divine benevolence.

God, Evolution, and Evil's Mystery

Julian Fernandes

1.1 Methodological Considerations

The approach to the subject of Evolution, Suffering and the God of the Bible is situated in relation to the taxonomy offered by Neil Messer (2007). Messer considers five possible options.

- o **Option 1**: Only science contributes to the account, and the contribution of Christian doctrine is dismissed.

  This option has no bearing on this work as it is, primarily, a theological work that discusses a scientific given—that of Evolutionary Theory.

- o **Option 2:** Both science and Christian doctrine contribute to the account; its shape is determined by the scientific contribution, and the input from Christian doctrine must be adjusted to fit the outlines determined by the scientific contribution.

  This approach cannot be the one taken here. It is Christian doctrine that is the determining factor—for it is with Christian doctrine that the challenge presently lies.

Option 3: Both science and Christian doctrine contribute, and neither has sole control over the shape of the account.

This option is partly acceptable. However, as conservative Christian beliefs are based on Scripture and tradition—that which has been affirmed by the conciliar creeds, as a reliable and, indeed, plausible account of the history of God's interaction with mankind—Scripture rather than scientific interpretation should have the final word. This is not to suggest that the evolutionary paradigm may be deficient but rather that it is a matter of doctrine over science; this is of particular importance as it is likely that, as scientific paradigms develop, the more 'accurate or more reliable model' will be accepted as being superior to the prevailing paradigm. Ideas change and paradigms may change along with those ideas.

God, Evolution, and Evil's Mystery

Julian Fernandes

Faith on the other hand does not depend on scientific verification but on adherence to the doctrine revealed in Scriptures and attested by the great councils of the Church.

Option 4: Both science and Christian doctrine contribute; the shape of the account is determined by Christian doctrine, and the scientific contribution is critically appropriated to that doctrinally shaped account. *This is crucial for this thesis—this particular type of encounter'—in which both science and Christian doctrine contribute to the account, its shape being determined by Christian doctrine, and the scientific contribution being critically appropriated to that doctrinally shaped account...' (60)* [1]

- **Option 5**: Only the contribution of Christian doctrine is admitted, the scientific contribution being denied or dismissed.

  This option is not relevant to this research project, since, in broad terms, the scientific relevance of an evolutionary narrative is not in question.

The author's Christian persuasion is summed up by the following:

- That Scripture (The Bible) is the final authority in all matters of faith and doctrine (sola Scriptura). It is not, however, advocated that the Scriptures are the product of 'divine dictation'—to quote Alister McGrath: "Just as Christ's divinity does not abrogate Christ's human nature, so the divine authorship of Scripture does not abolish its human authorship." (1993, 55)
- It is appreciated that 'no one proposition' may express all the truth but the notion that there is, therefore, no likelihood of any such truths is not denied. The author advocates belief in the propositional nature of

---

[1] For Messer this doctrinally shaped account can be found in the theology of Karl Barth.

God, Evolution, and Evil's Mystery
Julian Fernandes

Scripture e.g. 'Jesus Christ is Lord'; 'Humans are Sinful'; 'Jesus' death atones for human sin'; 'There is Judgement'. (Groothius 2000, 117) . "...the Christian gospel tells how for the world's redemption God entered into history,...'the eternal came into time, the kingdom of heaven invaded the realm of earth, in the great events of the incarnation, crucifixion, and resurrection of Jesus the Christ." (Bruce 1960, 7-8)

- The truth of Christian doctrine does not depend solely on personal belief or on the beliefs of the community of faith; it is true whether or not anyone adheres to its propositions.

- The importance of personal encounter/experience of God is a given though it is not advocated that experience is the sole witness of the work of God, or that it should have pre-eminence as the principal means of witness of the individual believer or of the community of faith.

Fundamental to this approach to the subject of evolutionary theodicy is the belief that the Testaments of the Bible are trustworthy in all things essential for faith. Gordon Wenham says (1987), regarding the problem of the received wisdom of the distant past and of the (post) modern present, that:

If it is correct to view Genesis 1-11 as an inspired retelling of ancient oriental traditions about the origins of the world—with a view to presenting the nature of the true God as one, omnipotent, omniscient, and good as opposed to the fallible, capricious, weak deities who populated the rest of the ancient world; if further it is concerned to show that humanity is central in the divine plan, not an afterthought; if finally it wants to show that man's plight is the product of his own disobedience and indeed is bound to worsen without divine intervention, Genesis 1-11 is setting a picture of the world that

God, Evolution, and Evil's Mystery
Julian Fernandes

is at odds both with the polytheistic optimism of ancient Mesopotamia and the humanistic secularisation of the (post) modern world. (Wenham 1987, .iii)

In the introduction to his book 'The Lost World of Genesis One' (2009) John, H. Walton says of the Old Testament, that "...it is God's revelation of himself to Israel and secondarily through Israel to everyone else." (7) Walton affirms the distinctiveness of the biblical literature when compared to other contemporary writings. Indeed Walton suggests that to compare the Old Testament to the literature of the ancient world is not, "...to assume that we expect to find similarity at every point." (Walton, 10). The Bible is, as Walton states, distinctive —in that it does reveal the nature and character of God. Moreover, Scripture is, as the apostle Paul makes clear in his letter to Timothy"...breathed out by God and profitable for teaching..."(2 Timothy 3:16). We advocate that it is the case that though the Bible uses various literary devices (metaphors, similes etcetera) this does not imply that it conveys indecisive language or that it does not include historical narrative[2]. It is also the case that although the Bible is not a textbook of science it informs us of the relation of God to the cosmos and to human beings. This does not mean that the Bible is offering some kind of 'scientific treatise' from which we can deduce equations. It means that Scripture reveals

---

[2] 'We know that the earth does not rest on literal foundations or pillars made of stone, concrete, or steel. We can therefore see that the words 'foundations' and 'pillars' are used in the metaphorical sense. However, it needs to be emphasised once more that the metaphors stand for realities. God the creator has built certain very real stabilities into the planetary system that will guarantee its existence so long as is necessary to fulfil his purposes. Science has been able to show us that the earth is stable in its orbit over long periods of time, thanks in part to the obedience of gravity to an inverse square law, to the presence of the moon, which stabilises the tilt of the earth's axis...' (Lennox 2011, 33)

certain truths but not others. Examples of such truths would be the essential [high] calling of humankind in God's creative purposes, and the redeeming work of Christ—and of God's immanent, cruciform relationship with his creation throughout the history of the cosmos.[3]

In addition to the above, the following commitments are an essential part of the argument given here in this thesis:

i.   That God is sovereign over the universe and all that functions within it: That this sovereign God is not to be confused with lesser gods—demiurges etc. Moreover, that the sovereign God has allowed evil to exist on earth so that evil is ultimately defeated.

ii.   That the emergence of creatures with the 'will to choose within the created order was a major part of God's goal for the creation.
The notion/possibility of the absence of Free-Will in advanced, sentient beings such as mankind would be in contradistinction to the character of the God who is the ultimate expression of personality and unity.

iii.   That the Goodness of God is coterminous with the justice of God. And the Justice of God entails God's *desire* to 'deliver from evil' rather than to exert a 'compensatory' form of justice—though God's ultimate justice must prevail in whatever form God so chooses.

---

[3] In addition to these there is the personal experience of the life changing power of Jesus Christ—through the Spirit of the Triune God. It is acknowledged however that experience may or may not, in real terms, verify the benevolence of God outside of that personal testimony .Indeed, it may be the case that personal testimonies offer varied definitions of 'realised' benevolence'. Nevertheless the personal experience of coming to Christ, in the author's case from atheism, most certainly had 'real' consequences: causes and effects.

iv.   Furthermore the argument in this thesis is that the laws of physics (as presently understood) are fundamental to God's creation of the cosmos and of the ensuing evolution of biological life forms—that it was God's preordained purpose that an evolutionary process should be the means through which God would bring about his eternal purposes [ultimately] at the eschaton.

1.2 Good & Evil

Psalm 19:1 says, "The heavens declare the glory of God, and the sky above proclaims his handiwork." Psalm 50:6, "The heavens declare his righteousness, for God himself is judge!" The universe is a glorious display of God's infinite power and of God's intricate handiwork. From an aesthetic perspective it could be said that biological evolution *per se* is wonderfully creative. Biological evolution is both a beautiful and a seemingly merciless system. Evolution could be described as the product of mindless 'opportunity' or of a merciless cosmic sadist. Whatever adjective or adjectival phrase one might use when describing the 'vista', process and effects of evolution, the argument here is that evolution is the only possible means through which God could have brought the genesis and telos of His creation. The view of both Robin Attfield (**2006**) and Christopher Southgate (**2008**)—is, indeed, that the values of such a process do outweigh the disvalues—that God's goodness is not an illusion but an actuality. However, differentiating between that which can be, justifiably, regarded as 'good' and that which constitutes 'evil' is an essential exercise for theodicy; this we do in the following section.

1.2.1 Good

God, Evolution, and Evil's Mystery
Julian Fernandes

Karl Bridges **(1997)** states that God's goodness is a bedrock truth of Scripture and that, "…although we might discuss God's goodness in some abstract philosophical sense, in Scripture his goodness appears most clearly in his dealings with people. He is not only good in general, but he is good *to us*." [4] **(Bridges 1997)** Goodness in its very essence, is 'God'. God is 'Good'. Jesus' command to 'love God with all our heart, soul, mind' (Matthew 22:37) is due to the fact that the God of the Judeo/Christian Scriptures *is* goodness personified—is indeed nothing other than love itself (1.John 4). Indeed, would it be possible to offer genuine love and worship to a deity that was a contradiction in terms? McCabe **(2010)** suggests that we cannot say merely that God is good but that God is goodness or that goodness is God: "In the end, what is common to good things is not that they share a characteristic but that they share a creator." **(3)**

1.2.2 Evil

The effects of 'evil' in this document are defined as the manifestation of 'harms' that are deemed to be contrary to the nature of goodness. McCabe states that, according to Aquinas, evil is a lack of good—a certain kind of absence **(60)**. "The word 'evil' signifies what St Thomas calls 'a sort of absence of good'….(*quaedam absentia boni*), because to say that goodness is absent is not always to say that something is lacking in the properties that make it good…" **(McCabe, 60)** Aquinas cites the example of 'a room lacking the goodness of a tree'; which simply means that there is no tree in the room. One might, of course, prefer that there were a tree in the room but its presence is not an essential part of the room.

---

[4] Bridges' view though seems to suggest a kind of subjective outcome that indicates an 'all is well' in a kind of: 'God is obliged to give every human (First World—at least) the most fulfilled, enjoyable/happy, existence/experience possible'. These things can, of course, define 'good outcomes' for those benefitting from such a subjective view of goodness but cannot be allowed to hijack the definition of God's absolute goodness. Moreover, it does not take into consideration suffering among other species and may, therefore, be considered too anthropocentric.

However, if the goodness of a tree were lacking in a tree then this absence may indicate deprivation or negation. Ergo, to lack something that is essential to the normal functionality of any living creature would be considered the opposite to a good outcome.

Norman Geisler (1974) suggests, along with Augustine et el, that evil is not a substance—it has no positive nature; but the loss of 'the good' is to be considered 'evil'. Geisler goes on to say that if evil were a substance, it would be good—since evil does not possess a nature of its own. "Evil does not subsist in itself; it lives only in another. It is an 'ontological parasite'...If one asks what is the cause of evil willing, Augustine replies, ' What cause of willing can there be which is prior to willing...? Either 'will' is itself the first cause of sin, or the first cause [a free creature] is without sin.[5]" (338-339) We absolutely concur with this view. Angels and men are both are created by God, though Angels, being incorporeal and extra-terrestrial, need not be considered 'products' of any evolutionary 'pathway'. Both were created with Free-Will, i.e. the will to make choices. It is these [wrong] choices that produce the potential for the absence of good outcomes—the occurrence of harmful outcomes. We refer here to the outcomes of free-will choices rather than to harmful outcomes proceeding from natural consequences, such as predation etc. Of course natural causes bring about Aquinas' privation as an exceedingly regular occurrence.

Tina Beattie says that Thomas Aquinas's view of morality makes humans responsible for their actions and that, "... there is no other excuse, in terms of an evil force manipulating our wills...unless we are suffering from some lack or

---

[5] Augustine, Two Souls: Against the Manichaeans, X; On Free Will I,I,1: III, xvii,49.

defect of our natural rational faculties that diminishes our responsibility, we are accountable for what we intentionally do or fail to do." (**Beattie 2012**)

She adds that Aquinas's view of moral responsibility—*for conscious agents with the will to do*—(our italics) confronts us with the question that was asked by Rabbi Eliezer Berkovits: "not where was God in Auschwitz, but where was man?" (**2012**) This may apply to both men and angels. This we want to distinguish from what Christopher Southgate refers to when he talks of harms that arise, not because of the decisions of men or angels but as a natural part of the cycle of life—'evolutionary evil' (**2008, 41**), that branch of natural evil that involves harms to creatures that has no human or angelic cause but rather seem to form part of the 'natural' processes of evolution. Southgate is correct regarding—what is generally perceived to be the major hurdle regarding the goodness and omnipotence of God—evolutionary evil. Indeed, this is the major 'Problem of Evil' but it is not the only source of harms—as if there were no other contenders that may be allowed to 'shoulder the blame', as shall be argued in Part Two of this thesis.

2. Creation & Goodness

2.1 Goodness in the Hebrew Scriptures

In this section the use of the word 'good' in Scripture is considered in reasonable detail ,in particular with regards to its use in the Genesis narrative[s]—how this word is ascribed to the God of the Bible and to his creation. In looking at the Genesis creation narrative (Genesis 1:1-2:3) C. J. Collins notes that the author of Genesis refers to God looking back at what he had created and stating that "behold, it was *very good*" (1:31). Collins, referring to Thomas Aquinas (2001, 82) writes that he [God] brought things into being—and that his goodness might be communicated to his creatures, and be represented by them. Yamauchi (2003) outlines five areas of 'good' *(tōv)* practical, abstract, quality, moral, and technical (2003). Melvin Tinker (2010) refers to the use of the word 'good' *(tōv)* and the conditioning of the word in context—suggesting that:

> ...while the word has many shades of meaning, ranging from 'useful to 'beautiful' to 'valuable', the meaning of the word in any particular case will be conditioned, to a large extent, by its immediate context. It can certainly mean 'aesthetically good' and need not mean 'perfection'...in the context of Genesis 1 the meaning is best taken as 'efficient'...This interpretation leaves room for the idea of a creation which is perfectly in line with what the creator intended but which is less than absolutely perfect,..."
> (Tinker, 49).

Ronald E. Osborn (2014) suggests that, as unsettling as it may be for some readers to discover, nowhere in Genesis is the creation described as 'perfect', "God declares his work to be good or **_tob_** at each stage and finally very good **_tob me 'od_** at its end. Elsewhere in The Hebrew Bible **_tob me 'od_** describes qualities of beauty, worthiness or fitness for a purpose but never absolute moral or ontological perfection." (29) In his comments on Genesis 1:31 Umberto Cassuto states that:

> ...we have here, at the conclusion of the story of creation, a more elaborate and imposing statement that points to the general harmony prevailing in the world of the Almighty. On the previous days the words that it was good were applied to a specific detail; now God saw everything that He had made, the creation in its totality, and He perceived that not only were the details, taken separately, good, very good, but that each one

harmonized with the rest; hence the whole was not just good, but very good.(Cassuto, 59-60)

It would seem, *prima facie,* most incongruous if the state of affairs Cassuto describes could be that of the 'genesis' of the evolutionary process but that would be to miss the point—for the Genesis narrative (1:31) states that, on the sixth day, "God saw everything he had made, and behold, it was very good." The question is: Would it have really been a time for rejoicing for an [omnipotent & omniscient] creator with any semblance of morality in his character?

It is clear from the Genesis text that God concluded, on the sixth day, that the creation was, indeed, 'very good'. The question arises as to how this 'very goodness' can apply to evolutionary creation? The key, we suggest, is in the literary function of the, "And God said" phrases—sometimes referred to as 'divine fiats'—occurring, as they do, at least nine times in chapter one of Genesis. Alan Hayward (1985) suggests that though the text doesn't tell us, there is a suggestion in the Job narrative that the audience of God's creative declarations may have been angels (Job 38:4-7). Hayward's point is that God does not see things the way man sees them and that, to God, "...the fiats are real; once the word is spoken, the deed is certain to follow. He commanded, and at once he saw—in his mind's eye, so to speak...from the perspective of Heaven it seems that foreordaining something is tantamount to creating it." (Hayward 1985, 174-175) It is in this sense that God can conclude—and that the author of Genesis can record—that the creation was, is and will be, 'Very Good'.

Making reference to the laws of physics, in particular the Second Law of Thermodynamics, Hayward comments that the Second Law does not denote a

God, Evolution, and Evil's Mystery
Julian Fernandes

universe where things have gone wrong but that, "It characterizes a universe where energy transfers can occur, and consequently where things can *happen*—in other words, a 'very good' universe." (Hayward 1985, 184) A world where the Second law did not operate would be, in Hayward's opinion, stagnant. Southgate (2008, 1) refers to the beautiful rhythms of the first chapter of the Hebrew Bible that culminate in the assertion that what God had made was 'very good'. Southgate (2008) however points out that humans have always known that the creation contained 'violence and pain' and accepts that there is a real problem in affirming with Genesis 1:31 that this creation is "very good" (14). He nevertheless holds that creation is good: "—in its propensity to give rise to great values of beauty, diversity, complexity, and ingenuity of evolutionary strategy." (15) Southgate makes clear nevertheless that these kinds of values do not of themselves act as justification for creation by means of evolution [by natural selection]. We agree with Southgate—that creation's propensity to give rise to 'great values' is a 'good'. The view here though is that God's 'very good' refers not to the beginnings of the creation [process], but to the whole of God's planned intentions for the creation—the 'alpha and omega'. In other words, God sees, in his mind's eye, the whole picture and it is this that is 'very good'. For God, surely, sees the beginning from the end and rejoices in the fact that 'Creation' is, de facto, very good. And this de facto good is not because 'the ends justify the means' but rather that 'the means' (the evolutionary process) is the only possible way for God to bring about an end that not only justifies the creator but that brings, at the eschaton, the best of possible outcome for all creatures—even Southgate's 'Pelican Heaven (2008, 85)'

Richard Swinburne argues that a perfectly good God would seek to do many good actions and no bad actions, and that, "good actions often derive their goodness

God, Evolution, and Evil's Mystery
Julian Fernandes

from bringing about states of affairs which are intrinsically good, that is good because of what they are and not because of how they were brought about or what they cause." (Swinburne 1998, 50). Understanding what is meant by goodness is crucial for the question of theodicy. Swinburne's comments are especially relevant regarding evolutionary theodicy and bear on the question of what the Bible means by 'good'.Jürgen Moltmann states that:

> The verdict on creation—that it was 'very good' does not mean that it was in the Greek sense perfect and without any future; the Hebrew means that it was fitting, appropriate, corresponding to the Creator's will. The accounts of the creation-in-the-beginning do not as yet talk about a creation in the glory of God. Only the Sabbath of creation is more than 'very good'. It is hallowed, sanctified and therefore points to creation's future glory. The Sabbath is, as it were, the promise of future consummation built into the initial creation." (1996, 264)

Moltmann's comments are insightful in that he offers, here, a rationale for past events and future 'glories' but without committing himself to a true definition of 'goodness'—apart from it (creation) being, at its inception, 'hallowed' and 'sanctified'. Moltmann's definition, if we have understood him correctly, will not totally suffice as he does not appear to align himself with any clear definition of 'the good' of creation. The question arises: Was it good or not? Our answer to that is that it was 'very good'. Herbert McCabe (2010, 59), working from the thought of Thomas Aquinas, argues that, "God whose essence is not potential with respect to existence, and which therefore does not constitute a limiting context for transcendental words *(i.e.goodness)*, we can say not merely that God is good but that God is goodness or that goodness is God. " For Aquinas, to have a concept of goodness in the sense in which we have a concept would be to comprehend God. We take this to mean that God, in God's self, is the ultimate expression of goodness.

2.2 'Good' as opposed to 'Bad'

God's purposes for His creation, it is reasonable to assume, are 'good'—good, that is, as opposed to: evil, wicked, corrupt, ruthless and unscrupulous—in the ethical sense 'good and not bad'. John Swinton (2007) refers to Martin Buber who held that good was the product of striving for truth and beauty: " 'Such goodness', Buber believed, does not occur accidentally, rather; 'it emerges from intentional practices of caring about and paying attention to particular noble goals.'" (Swinton, 180-181) It is indeed these 'noble' goals of God that we seek to comprehend. Collins (2006, 69) suggests that the goodness of creation implies that the result of God's creative endeavours were pleasing to God; God thought that the results were *good. Collins* concludes: "To affirm that the creation is 'good' then, is to affirm that God takes delight in it and that man <u>at his best </u>will do so as well." (70) Ernest Lucas states that the meaning of the goodness in the Creation Narrative is clear from the context: "...it pleased God. It pleased him because it reflected something of himself...The fact that it pleased God also means that <u>it was free of evil</u>, which becomes the major cause of the absence of *shalom* after the *[Genesis]* fall." (Lucas, 172). If, therefore the creation outcome pleased God, because of the efficient (*tov*) nature of the creation, we can conclude that the outcome is good even though this 'good' may not, presently, be fully comprehended by lesser beings. Terence Penelhum notes (1990) that in calling God 'good', one is not merely applying to God some 'general epithet of commendation', with no ancillary commitment on what he might be expected to do. Penelhum suggests that, "it would be vacuous to apply the concept of goodness without a fairly detailed idea of what these standards are—the standards which the speaker must regard as applying to himself." (Penelhum, 75).[6]

2.3 Goodness and its implications for an Evolutionary Theodicy

Gregory Boyd (2001) refers to the work of Howard Bloom, who describes the creation in terms of it being 'The Lucifer Principle', that is: nature abhorring evil and yet seemingly embracing it, "For Bloom, the Lucifer principle is simply part of the way things are. But no one who accepts that the cosmos was created by an all-good and all-powerful God can accept this." (2001, 245) Boyd affirms that creation displays, "...remarkable purposes and design, enough to proclaim the wisdom of a grand designer (Romans 1:20)." (245) Boyd though qualifies this by stating that the world also displays the antithesis of unified purpose and design. Boyd's points are relevant to a perspective that <u>cannot</u> accept that an omnipotent God could have allowed the prevailing state of affairs to pertain. However, what is advocated in this thesis is that the creation, with all the values and disvalues, is indeed the world God intended from eternity and is, until the eschaton, an unfinished creation.

John Polkinghorne (1991, 99) suggests that the goodness referred to by the author of Genesis should be understood in terms of what Polkinghorne calls 'fruitful potentiality' rather than some kind of initial perfection. So, for Polkinghorne,

---

[6] We may identify with the notion of this 'goodness' though we are likely to demand evidence of it on the creator's part. However, we, more often than not, fail miserably to give evidence of it in our own lives though our seeking evidence of it in the life of God is not misplaced—for we are the Imago Dei.

there was no perfect state but only the potential for fruitfulness. This does allow for (positive) unknown (fruitful) outcomes—the kind of potential for what God may bring about at the 'eschatological finale'. However, Polkinghorne's reference to potentiality leaves in doubt any outcome that God may, somehow, bring about, through the evolutionary 'creative' process. Rowan Williams is more explicit in his interpretation of the Genesis narrative, allowing for the fruitful eventuality of an evolutionary process, and suggests that Creation in the classical sense does not involve some uncritical idea of God's monarchy—rather that, "...the absolute freedom ascribed to God in creation means that God cannot make a reality that then needs to be actively governed, subdued, bent to the divine purpose away from its natural source." According to Williams, if God creates freely, God does not need the power of a sovereign; what is, is from God. God's sovereign purpose is what the world is becoming. (R. Williams 2000, 69) Williams' view allows for the introduction of a lesser 'deity'—a 'god' to suit a view that leaves little room for the existence of the God of Scripture. Williams' view as with Polkinghorne's, seems to leave everything open to the 'mystically-sovereign-purposes' of God. Well, we know a little of what the world was and has been, and we are informed by scientific prediction as to what the world might become. However, it is the Biblical revelation that offers us a 'God's eye view' of what God has in mind for the (biological) by-products of any evolutionary process. The tension here is obvious: should the creation have been completed sometime back in the distant (or not so distant) past then there would not have been a process taking 13.7 billion years (so far) to complete; it would have been a 'finished' work and there would be no question of God lacking power or needing to relinquish power in order to allow for a more intimate connection with the creation process. However, the insights of Williams and Polkinghorne are helpful in that they point us to a future in which God's absolute goodness may realise vindication.

But, it is not sufficient enough to philosophise about an unknown future—even when supporting the notion of the goodness of the God of Scripture. There is, surely, something more to offer for those seeking answers. The search for a plausible theodicy is, indeed, the raison d'être of this thesis and is addressed in the 'Eight-Step-Argument' in part two.

2.3.1   Distinctions

Most, post Darwinian, attempts at a defence or theodicy, avoid any notion of the prevailing state of affairs being the result of any major shift in the order of creation; few, if any, offer an Adamic Fall as the reason for the existence of predation, plague and parasitism though some offer an Angelic Fall as an alternative—a fall that brought about and continues to bring about major negative effects on the Creation—effects that God is not responsible for, but that He allows. The majority of these defences/theodicies adhere to a theistic-evolutionary perspective—William Dembski's (2009) effort being an exception/variation.

In this chapter we looked, in reasonable detail, at the notion of 'goodness' as applied to Scripture. We argued that the creation is good in the sense of it being the best possible creation that would enable its creator to bring about a best possible state of affairs at the eschaton—a pathway to an eschatological ideal. Moreover, we argued that the creation should not, in spite of it producing harms, be considered anything other than good as Scripture affirms (Genesis 1:31)—a Sovereign God's 'very good' over the creation.

3. Changes to the traditional/
Biblical view of the attributes of God

3.1   What of GOD?

The God portrayed and 'defended' in this thesis is the God of the Judeo/Christian Scriptures. A God whose eternity, Peter Sanlon (2014) describes as a qualitatively different kind of existence to the one of his creatures (87)."Being outside of time does not mean that God cannot know what happens inside of time, nor that he cannot interact with a temporal order. Quite the opposite! It does, of course, shape the way he does these things." (88) As Sanlon makes clear in the same passage, "It would perhaps be odd for him to create something he could not interact with. Similarly God created time. It is part of the created order. And though God is not himself temporal, he can interact with, and know all that occurs in, the times he has made. Indeed, precisely because God is not temporal he has perfect knowledge of all events in time." (88) This God is not to be confused with any other ideas/notions/theologies or philosophies of God—either pre-modern, modern or post-modern—as shall be made clear throughout the development of the argument.

In this section we, briefly, address, what may be considered the 'straw men' (demeaning caricatures) of modern and post-modern attempts at lessening the culpability of the classical 'image' of God in the light of evolutionary theory—and also in the light of contemporary religious and philosophical notions of the reality of God. The views offered here are considered incontrovertibly necessary to the defence of the God of the Bible against other notions and ideas that *may be seen* to better fit the evolutionary paradigm but that only serve to remove the problem by the substitution of the God of Scripture with a lesser 'deity'.

3.1.1 Constraints on God

Should God be limited in his ability to produce or concoct the best possible plans for fulfilling his creative objectives, God would not be omnipotent. Christopher Southgate (**2008, 29**) argues that the sort of universe we have, in which complexity emerges in a process governed by thermodynamic necessity and Darwinian natural selection, is the only sort of universe that could give rise to all that the earth has produced. To affirm evolutionary process as being 'the only way' through which God could achieve his objectives one has to assume that God was unable (lacked the ability) to bring about his creative objectives without this astronomical/biological framework or that God's use of such a process was the best possible means through which God could bring about the best of possible outcomes. This is, a similar point to the one noted in Alexander, that sees biology as a 'package deal' (**2008, 279**). If biology should be a 'stand-alone-package-deal' that has no significance other than it being the product of creative genius, it is reasonable to suppose that the creator's benevolent characteristics be called into question—unless there is more to the story other than God's desire to create. This is, of course, assuming that there has been an intentional pathway within the evolutionary process—otherwise there would be no reason to suppose that any such future outcomes could be considered anything other than random outcomes within the naturally selective process of evolution. Jeff Astley (**2009**) asks whether or not God could have ordered nature differently and then answers his own question by saying, 'perhaps not'. Astley goes on to say however that materiality inevitably involves imperfection—a tendency to disorder, decay, fragility, and mortality (**167**). Astley's point is significant as it is the case that the accusation against the 'designer God' is often that of incompetence—that the design is simply under par or faulty. Ergo, God is either impotent or fails to meet the necessary criteria or the presuppositions of the complainant. This assertion is false as we shall argue in part two of this thesis; indeed Keith Ward (**1990**) is correct when he refers to 'natural' evil as an inevitable consequence of this kind of world, which we shall argue in part two, is a necessary kind of world.

3.1.2 'A Question of Ontological Veracity'

In this section we briefly address the notion of 'God' as the ground of being rather than as a determinate entity.

Should the term 'God' refer only to a 'ground of being' first cause—a first cause that defies description or a 'first cause' that may be loosely described as 'nature'—then there would be no case to answer as there would be no personal creative-agent against whom a charge may be brought. For should the term 'God' refer only to a 'ground of being' first cause—a first cause that defies description or that may be loosely described as 'nature'—then there is no case to answer— for there is, indeed, no personal agent that may be found guilty of failure of any sort. The notion of a 'Ground of Being', presumably, thought by its advocates, to deal with the problem of natural evil, does nothing of the sort apart from demeaning the God of the Bible. However, it is such a view that is commonly espoused by philosophical theologians such as Wesley Wildman.

Wesley Wildman says (2007, 167) that any notion of 'ultimate reality' is bizarre but adds that 'most theologians and a few philosophers are captivated by such (ultimate reality) speech' and that they even choose it while understanding its 'final futility'. In his section on 'Determinate-Entity Theism' Wildman, regarding this alleged futility, asks (170) what kind of entity the divine reality really is?

God, Evolution, and Evil's Mystery

Julian Fernandes

His conclusion is that the God of the Bible seems to be made in the image of its authors. In short, God's determinate nature is known in our longings. Everything else we say theologically must serve this overridingly important version of ultimate reality, and this becomes the crucial criterion of determinate-entity theism. Wildman's views seem to have little to do with any perceived notion of the goodness of the Triune God of Scripture, as Wildman's picture of God bears no resemblance whatsoever to this God. He writes:

> Speaking of God as the ground of being removes the possibility of proposing a divine character that is profoundly different from the character of the world. This is its chief theological difference from its competitors. Determinate-entity theism requires a divine goodness that our best scientific vision of the cosmos does not easily support and so positively requires some ontological distance between God and the world and a layer of theological explanation for why the world is the way it appears to be despite the purported impeccability of God's moral character...Ground-of-being theism needs neither to explain a discrepancy nor to distinguish among events to articulate the divine nature.
> (W. Wildman 2007, 281)

Wildman's views are clearly expressed. Indeed, it would seem that the notion of God as a 'determinate entity' creates enormous philosophical questions—especially with regard to the problem of [natural] evil. It is, of course, possible that the God revealed in the Bible is a figment of the imaginative wishful thinking of latter day Homo Sapiens—particularly the authors of the Old Testament. Wildman states (282) that the 'divine goodness' described in the Scriptures is a difficult fit with the apparent evidence. However, it is striking that many

God, Evolution, and Evil's Mystery
Julian Fernandes

---

distinguished theologians and philosophers are content to hold to a more classical approach. Keith Ward (2008) comments that to call God good is to say that God actualises within himself the best of all possible perfections—moreover, Ward suggests that, "If such a God produces a universe like this, then God remains good, whatever the universe is like. A supremely good God might, then, necessarily create this universe, or some universe with similar characteristics." (Ward, 92) By 'necessarily' we take it (though Ward doesn't state this) that the sovereign God chose to create this universe in order to bring about the best of possible circumstances, *i.e.*, the 'best possible world'. This does not imply lesser capabilities on God's part but rather that this world is, *de facto*, the best possible world—the world in which God's ultimate 'Good' purposes can be achieved.

As far as Biblical Theism is concerned, there should be no willingness to dilute God's attributes; however should there be any attempts at 'dilution' the most likely candidates would be those of omnipotence or benevolence. Should God be declared 'less than powerful' or 'not quite as powerful' as previously thought, the question of God's benevolence becomes less crucial. Omnipotence, however, remains crucial to any evolutionary theodicy that takes seriously the legitimacy of the biblical narratives. The 'God is not benevolent' view seeks to remove the notion of both evil and benevolence from the 'stage' but, nevertheless offers a reason for the existence of 'harms'. For proponents of this position, the argument is likely to be that God <u>does not have</u> the necessary characteristics that enable him to behave with consistent benevolence. Wildman gives an outline of the possibilities: Firstly, he makes clear his view that (a) a personal, benevolent, attentive, and active deity cannot create through evolution and (b) that therefore God the creator is not a personal, benevolent, attentive, and active deity. He states that we can preserve those affirmations symbolically (for whatever reason),

God, Evolution, and Evil's Mystery
Julian Fernandes

but goes on to say that, "... they no longer refer to a divine being with intentions and awareness, with feelings and intelligence, with plans and powers to act. Rather, they refer to the ground of being itself, to the creative and fecund power source *in the depths of nature*, to the value structures and potentialities that the world manifests. They refer to the God beyond God, which is to say the truly ultimate reality that hovers behind and beneath and beyond the symbolic gods we create and deploy to satisfy our personal needs, to make sense of our world, and to legitimate the exercise of social control." (W. Wildman 2011)

There is neither time or space to discuss Wildman's assertion that the God of the Bible could not have created through an evolutionary process, though we disagree entirely with his conclusions. We however accept that this does offer, to some extent, a challenge regarding providence within the evolutionary process. Wildman's 'god' though lacks 'substance' lacks any notion of benevolence— indeed lacks anything in real terms. Naturally, this 'god' cannot manifest personal concern for the products of any likely creative processes because this 'god' has no personality from which to proceed. Nevertheless, Wildman's alternative is somehow able to 'allow for' the transformation of the material in the cosmos that allowed for the evolution of the biosphere etc.

Wildman's apparent disillusionment with the classical notion of God has provoked him to strong language ; Clayton and Knapp (2007) make the following reference to Wildman's disdain, quoting him thus: "Frankly, and I say this with the utmost reverence, the personal God does not pass the test of parental moral responsibility. If God really is personal in this way, then we must conclude that God has a morally abysmal record of inaction or action."[7] (179-180)

Sigmund Freud's view (Nicholi 2002), that the very idea of 'an idealized Superman' in the sky is so patently infantile and so foreign to reality seems, most likely, to stem from a total miscomprehension—even caricature of the God of the Bible. It is no doubt the case that some may naively interpret the biblical notion of God in the way Freud expresses, but some (an increasing number even) may, due to this kind of reasoning or lack of a plausible notion of the God of the Bible, wish to find an alternative 'god'—this, we suggest, is totally the wrong direction to take as it leads to another path—a path void of any notion of 'God' whatsoever to anything other than an unworthy caricature of the God that Scripture reveals.

Wesley Wildman is of the opinion that ground-of-being theologies are important because of their denial that ultimate reality can 'possibly' be a determinate entity at all—and that this establishes a valuable theological contrast with determinate entity theisms. The 'ground-of-being' view of the 'personhood' of God as well as God's possible interaction with the world may, as Wildman suggests, produce a hopeful intellectual response to these pervasive evils. But, at the same time, this view favours philosophical logic over and above the revelation of Scripture. Wildman, we believe, is mistaken in his deliberations—his alternative 'deity' being unacceptable. It is unacceptable for two reasons. Firstly, as a result of his dissatisfaction/disappointment with the 'performance' of the God of the Bible Wildman offers an extra-biblical, pantheistic alternative. Secondly, the

---

[7] Wildman says, regarding the use of the word 'evil', that 'suffering is a more useful category than evil because suffering is more neutrally descriptive and does not prejudge the moral character of...[?] regarding natural disasters, predation and the like'. Here, Wildman may well be correct.

substituted, 'ground of being', alternative, apart from being unbiblical, fails to convince us that 'it' has any substance whatsoever. Regarding, the 'narrative to Scripture', Peter Sanlon says that, "...for the drama to be of any significance whatsoever there must be real actors in the play. If the metaphor of a drama has to be developed further, then it must be insisted that the scriptwriter is also real. The God who creates, speaks, directs, interacts and participates must be a real person before he can do any of these things. In the technical terminology, ontology is prior to revelation and salvation. Systematic theology recognises this, and asks the entirely appropriate questions 'What kind of being is he?' and, What may we know of him from his words and actions?'" (Sanlon 2014, 72)

God is the Triune 'determinate entity' who has created all things and who sustains all things for His 'good' purposes. Ergo, God is the ultimate ontological reality.

3.1.3   Process thought and Omnipotence

In this section we will briefly consider process theology as it applies to 'omnipotence'. Cobb & Griffin (1976, 69) state the dominant position of process theologians clearly enough when they pose the question of why evil exists when there is in existence, according to classical and biblical theology, a God with 'controlling power'—suggesting that, "... a major reason that Christian theism has clung on so long to the notions of God as a Controlling Power is that thereby it can assure believers that God's will, despite appearances, is victorious—for the sake of this assurance it has risked seeing God as the author of needless suffering and even moral evil. It has risked the implicit denial of human freedom and the rebellion of humanistic atheism." (Process Theology, 118)

God, Evolution, and Evil's Mystery
Julian Fernandes

There is a something to be said for this critique. However, the above depiction is an extreme caricature and it is not the picture of sovereignty that is anywhere near to that adhered to by the author of this thesis—or to that even of Open Theism which offers freedom without, mostly, denying the overall sovereignty of God (Pinnock 2000)[8]. Indeed, the Process view offers a rather simplistic view of sovereign reality as it does not allow any means with which to comprehend any notion of ontological veracity for this alleged 'ground of being' other than as some kind of nebulous force akin to that of pantheism. Indeed, it does not offer anywhere near sufficient reason to replace the God of Scripture with any 'straw man' scenario in the form of dialectical hypothesis. Wildman (2006, 274) acknowledges the difficulty in that whatever God is, on the process account, it is exceedingly resistant to anthropomorphic modelling, "and certainly nothing like the personal God of so many sacred texts and religious pieties". Wildman 's summary accurately describes the problem from both perspectives.

The God of process theology is considered to be a God that does not abuse, or 'coerce' but persuades—throughout nature and in living beings. The God of process theology cannot override free will; it is not that he will not but rather that he cannot (cannot as in does not have the potency to so do). According to Griffin (Lubarsky & Griffin 1996), the redefining of the omnipotence of God may be the solution that dissolves the problem of evil as there is no likelihood of culpability on the part of this particular notion of God.

---

[8] According to Clark Pinnock, "God as the creator of *the world* (italics ours) can make the kind of world he likes—in this case a world with free creatures in it...God exercises power in ways appropriate to the creation project...He gives creatures the room decides things and binds himself to the promises he makes. Thus God exercises sovereignty by sharing power not by dominion...God uses omnipotence to 'free' and not enslave...It takes omnipotence to create and manage freedom..." (Pinnock 2000, 93,94,95)

God, Evolution, and Evil's Mystery
Julian Fernandes

Any possibility of continued adherence to the biblical view of omnipotence is ruled out as is made clear from the following quotation from Griffin:

> Because our universe was created out of chaos rather than out of absolute nothingness, so that creative power is inherent in the world (as well as in God), the creatures' twofold creative power of self-determination and efficient causation cannot be cancelled, overridden, or completely controlled by God. On this basis process philosophy denies the second premise in the argument…saying instead that although God is all-powerful —not only in the sense of being the supreme power of the universe but also in the sense of being perfect in power, having all the power one being could possibly have—God *cannot* unilaterally prevent all evil. If being 'all-powerful' is taken to mean being omnipotent in the sense of essentially having all the power, however, then process philosophy simply denies the first premise's assertion that a being worthy of the name God is all-powerful by definition. (Griffin 2001, 223-224)

Both the logic and implications of this kind of thinking are clear. There is, according to this view, in the world of matter—matter that pre-existed the emergence of God, an inherent creative capability out of which appears the process of evolution—a process that 'God' could not interfere with but only persuade. So it is from within the alleged 'inherent creative capability' of matter itself that the force of evolution manifests itself (*ex nihilo, nihil fit*)—and not out of the MIND of the God of Scripture—***ex nihilo***. Griffin states that God, though having all the power possible, does not possess 'ALL POWER' and therefore is not capable of preventing evil or of much else regarding the biological evolutionary process.[9] [10]

The idea that any such imagined requiredness could exist as a de facto state of affairs—'conjured up' as a more convenient replacement for the God of Biblical Theology—is hardly convincing. Moreover, the notion that ethical principles (or any other come to that) are likely to emanate from anything other than the actual character [Mind] of The God, who is by His very nature 'the ultimate good' is equally unconvincing. We are in agreement with Gregory Boyd (2001) who states that, "...unless God's essential nature is necessary and actual—apart from his interaction with the world, neither the enduring nature of God nor the contingent nature of the world can be rendered intelligible. God must be self-sufficient within himself, creating and relating to the world out of love instead of metaphysical necessity." (276) In the light of the problem of creaturely suffering the process 'alternative' may seem an attractive proposition—one that may fit in with some current understandings of reality, but it cannot be taken as the final word regarding the God of the Bible as it fails miserably to do justice to the character of that God. This view of God, helpfully, dissolves the problem of evil. A

---

[9] Madden & Hare (1987) conclude that the _process_ God is, "...unable to move toward an aesthetic end and without an enormous cost in pain (his own and others); he is apparently so weak that he cannot guarantee his own welfare. If he is that weak, obviously he is not able as a theistic God should be, to _ensure_ the ultimate triumph of an end of his choice."(29)

[10] In contra distinction to the views espoused by Griffin, Wildman et el, John Leslie (1989) suggests that, "Neoplatonism is [today] often expressed in such a formulae as that God is not a being but the Power of Being. On my interpretation, what dark sayings say that God is the world's ethical requiredness or, equivalently, that God is the creatively effective ethical need that there should exist a (good) world." (167)

God with restricted or limited ability can hardly be held responsible for failing to address the problem of suffering in any significant way. Indeed, this 'god', it could be said, cannot entertain any kind of 'planned intention'—vis a vis the creation of anything much—most certainly not creation ex nihilo. This God though could not be mistaken for the God of the Judeo/Christian Scriptures as this view of God is a step into the unknown and 'unknowable', and is not a God we could visualise and, most certainly is nothing like the Triune God of the Bible.

Paul Copan and William Lane Craig offer a helpful summary regarding the difference between 'abstract' and 'concrete' objects:

> We have seen that God, though immaterial and not spatio-temporal, would be classed by everyone as a concrete object in view of his being a personal causal agent. Perhaps that provides a clue to the distinction between concrete and abstract entities. It is virtually universally agreed that abstract objects, if they exist, are causally impotent; they do not stand in causal relations. Numbers, for example, do not effect anything. (Copan 2004, 168)

The following chapter offers a discussion of several relatively recent attempts at an evolutionary theodicy. Each of the views mentioned have wrestled with and have contributed to the work of seeking a plausible defence/theodicy in the post-Darwin world of science, philosophy and theology. These 'offerings' are insightful and helpful and have allowed for the development of the Eight-Step-Argument offered in this thesis.

4. Ideas that further the case for the omnipotence and benevolence of God—in the light of an evolutionary consensus:

In this section we consider the published works of William Dembski, John Haught, Michael Murray & Christopher Southgate (2007-2010) and that of Michael Lloyd (1998) that deal, particularly, with evolution and the problem of evil.

4.1 Evolution: God's response to rebellion

William Dembski (2009, 20) makes much of the attributes of God and rails against any attempts to restrict God's activity to the metaphysical, the biophysical or 'the present tense'. Dembski (50) asks why it is that, in the economy of the world whose creator is 'omnipotent, omniscient, and trans-temporal', should causes always precede effects? 'Clearly, such a Creator could act to anticipate events that have yet to happen. Moreover, those events could be the occasion (or 'cause') of God's prior anticipatory action.'

Dembski takes the Adamic Fall as a major event in the history of the world and offers a defence based on Genesis chapter three[11]. However, Dembski states that in arguing that the fall of mankind marks the entry of all evil into the world (both personal and natural evil) he makes no assumptions about the age of the Earth, the extent of evolution, or the prevalence of design. He does though state that

---

[11] Dembski (p146) refers to Adam and Eve as the initial pair of humans—as the progenitors of the whole human race; he furthermore suggests that they were specially created by God, and thus that they were not the result of an evolutionary process from primate or hominid ancestors.

the theodicy he develops, "...looks not to science but to the metaphysics of divine action and purpose." (10) In other words his concern is to offer a defence without particular deference to scientific opinion.[12]

Dembski states that the theodicy he is proposing gladly acknowledges that important similarities exist between humans and primates but he, nevertheless insists that far-reaching differences also exist, "...especially differences in cognitive and moral capacities, and that these represent a difference in kind and not, as Darwin and many contemporary evolutionists hold, merely a difference in degree." (161) Dembski's approach is one that maintains the uniqueness of the Imago Dei—that there is indeed something uniquely significant about the 'arrival' of early humans[13]. Here, we are in full agreement with Dembski. Dembski, though, addresses the problem of evil with a novel alternative to the traditional offerings. His major thrust is to do with what he terms 'retroactivity'.

> In contrast to theodicies that attempt to justify God's goodness by limiting God, I'm going to argue that full divine foreknowledge of future contingent propositions in fact helps to reconcile God's goodness with the existence of evil. By taking a retroactive approach to the Fall, which traces

---

[12] This is an opinion with which we are mostly in agreement with. However, though we take seriously the evolutionary perspective we do not allow it to dictate terms—as the problem of evil within the theistic-evolutionary-paradigm is not with the science but with the God of the Judeo/Christian Scriptures. It would matter little if there were no such God and no such Scriptures.

[13] Stephen Webb refers to Richard Middleton's (2005) position which, according to Webb has "...severed the anthropological implications of the imago from the cosmological...Instead, it should lead us to contemplate the cosmological significance of Jesus Christ, who is "the exact imprint of God's very being." (Hebrews 1:3). The cosmological provides the foundation for the anthropological... (2010, 287)

all evil in the world back to human sin (even the natural evil that predates human sin), the theodicy I develop preserves the traditional view that natural evil is a consequence of the Fall. (129-130)[14]

In essence, what Dembski proposes is that God, having foreseen the rebellion of humanity in the space-time continuum, brought into being the evolutionary programme of 'life, predation, parasitism, disease and death' as punishment for the 'future' disobedience of Adam and Eve. It was a kind of pre-emptive strike against the 'future' free-will behaviour of the two. Dembski consistently upholds the conservative evangelical argument regarding both the 'punishment' and the 'acquittal' and the consequential effects on God's 'good' creation—at least when it comes to the events prior to God's 'retro-proactivity'.

> Thus, just as the death and resurrection of Christ is responsible for the salvation of repentant people[15] throughout *all time,* so the Fall of humanity in the Garden of Eden is responsible for every natural evil throughout all time (Future, present, past, and distant past preceding the Fall). (110)

We agree with Dembski with regards to the salvific power of the cross of Christ. However, with regards his view that the Adamic fall brought about such an 'earth shattering' change in the creation, we disagree. Would God really have brought about such a drastic state of affairs—over the disobedience of the pair in the garden? Dembski, we feel, has introduced an unnecessary element into the

---

[14]Dembski points out (2009, 110) that a retroactive view of the fall was one of several (Christian) options proposed in the nineteenth century to explain pre-human suffering and death; Dembski refers as such to J. Dana (writing in 1853—prior to the Darwinian revolution).

[15] Dembski offers no explicit justification for the plight of animals—or indeed the 'created order' other than human beings.

argument—not so much the 'Fall' (though our view differs from his)—but the retroactive retribution that he introduces.

In offering this innovative approach Dembski does allow for God to be God, and does allow 'space' for biological evolution—its cycle of life, predation and death—without having to deal with the notion of there being no physical death before the disobedience of advanced hominids whenever the incident may have occurred in the space/time continuum.

Dembski's approach—though innovative and intriguing—offers a picture of God as being so taken up with anger and disappointment that he brings about a retroactive state of affairs that would have been totally unnecessary[16]; a state of affairs that punishes creatures for a sin that had not even occurred. Dembski's thesis seems to offer a God who punishes innocent creatures because of something that would happen long after their death.

4.2 'Making Sense of Evolution'

John Haught (2010) holds that the continuous evolution of life, from the initial protoplasm to the end of evolution (presumably the eschaton), continues to wind its autonomous way without any tangible sign of the divine agent—most certainly not that of a cosmic engineer 'tinkering' with project creation[17] [18].

---

[16] Does not the Genesis text (3:22-24) state that the pair were expelled from the garden and prohibited from partaking of the fruit of the tree of life? Moreover, did not God plant a 'garden in Eden' (2:8) in which he put (2:18) the man Adam? Is it not likely that outside of the confines of the garden—the biosphere continued to allow for the 'life-death cycle' of the evolutionary process? Moreover, Dembski's thesis seems to offer a God who punishes innocent creatures because of something that would happen long after their death

[17] Haught refers to such a possible scenario as being 'dead on delivery'. (2010, 63)

God, Evolution, and Evil's Mystery
Julian Fernandes

Haught, indeed, refers to the impressiveness of a divine maker of a 'self-creative' world and suggests that 'the divine maker of such a self-creative world is arguably much more 'impressive—hence worthier of human reverence and gratitude—than a 'designer' who moulds and micro-manages everything directly. (42) Haught makes reference to the work of Paul Tillich. Tillich held the view that nature had an inexhaustible dimension—and that this dimension allows theology to avoid what Haught refers to as 'the traps that occur whenever we wonder how God could possibly act or intervene in nature'. In answer to **the** question, 'What is really going on in nature?' Haught says that, "...if nature has an inexhaustible depth, we can respond to this question by differentiating reading levels, such as those of science and theology, without having to resort to fruitless speculation about how divine influence somehow 'hooks itself' into natural processes." (97) Haught's point here seems to be that there are different levels of 'interpretation' and that, to avoid wasting time with speculative reasoning—such as attempting to locate evidence for God's craftsmanship at the molecular level—theologians should leave science to the scientist—concentrating more on matters of theology. For Haught the important question is not how God acts in nature but how deep we are willing to look in our quest to understand 'what's really going on in the drama of life and *the cosmos'*. He refers to evolution as a *'still-unfinished drama rather than a factory of designs'* (57) and argues that accidents, natural selection and time are instances of the elements necessary to any dramatic story, and that focussing on evolution as a still-unfinished drama rather than a factory of designs is crucial. The question is: Where is this seemingly directionless,

---

[18] Haught holds to a form of Process Theology and thus states: *"...to those who object that process theology is hereby illegitimately redefining the idea of God's power in order to contrive a fit with neo-Darwinian theory, the reply is simply that no other conceptions of power is more consistent with the quite orthodox religious belief that God is infinite love."* (Haught, God After Darwin: A Theology of Evolution 2001, 42)

openly indefinable journey heading? Moreover, how is it possible for God to be responsible for the direction of the evolutionary process (in control of it in some tangible way), and therefore culpable?

Haught is aware that 'most readers' of Darwin's Origin of Species would consider that a 'do-nothing God' differs little from no God at all (43) but nevertheless describes God as, "...the inexhaustible dimension of depth beneath the surface of our lives and of nature." (91) He goes on to suggest that this God may seem absent or even non-existent since we have no evidence of depth in the scientific sense: "Darwin, in other words, has portrayed the life-story as a true adventure. Evolution is a risk-taking and extravagantly inventive drama. Alongside its lush creativity, there always exists the possibility of tragic outcomes, including abundant suffering and perpetual perishing. Haught suggests that, to Christians, there is something 'cruciform' about the whole drama of life. (63) There is 'something cruciform going on'. Indeed, the evolutionary process can be viewed as being 'a risk-taking and extravagantly inventive drama'. Some interpreters may wish to leave it there—'content' in their ignorance—disallowing the likelihood of God having any ultimate 'design' objective for His creation. Haught is correct of course when he claims that a 'theology of evolution' (83) is not interested in defending the idea of a 'designer God' per se, "...as this would only make us wonder why the 'designer' does not immediately eliminate the disorder of suffering in the drama of life." In other words: why would the designer make no effort to 'immediately' eliminate the effects of the bad design—should there have been a 'bad design' in the first place. We, along with Southgate and others do not hold the view that there ever was a 'bad design' or a malfunction within the universal law of physics—contrary to Adrian Hough's (2010) interesting idea of a 'flaw in the universe'.

God, Evolution, and Evil's Mystery

Julian Fernandes

Regarding evolutionary theory, Haught asks whether or not 'a theology of evolution' can, indeed, make sense of 'life's suffering'. His conclusion is that it cannot, **yet**, do so and he states that, if there ever was a question resistant to receiving a presently satisfying response, it is that of why the drama of life involves so much agony and loss. "To make ourselves receptive to any answer at all, however, we must be prepared to wait. Such is the requirement of faith." (83-84) Haught is, of course, correct—we can only speculate as we do not have all the answers; waiting is a requirement of faith (Hebrews Chapter 11). However, the Christian faith is based on both future revelation (what Scripture points to) and past (not too insignificant) events such as the incarnation and resurrection (what Scripture attests). Of course there are questions, scientific or otherwise, that humans, in spite of their persistent endeavours, will have no closure on. However, Haught, we maintain, is incorrect in his bleak analysis—as if Scripture gives no clue to the purposes of the God of creation. Indeed it does, as shall be obvious from the main argument of this thesis.

The language Haught uses is contemporary and it fits in well with current theistic-evolutionary views of craftsmanship rather than design. God's desire to produce the 'Greatest Show on Earth' (Dawkins 2009) may well be 'reason enough' for the existence of pain and suffering but this reasoning will not suffice to defend the benevolence of God. Whatever one makes of this kind of reasoning it is not sufficient enough to 'get God of the hook'—at least not the God whose benevolent character would, according to some, not have allowed such compromise. Haught's God, though, seems not to be in danger of needing any kind of defence.

4.3   'Nature Red in Tooth & Claw'

Michael Murray (2008) offers what he terms as a reasonable defence rather than actual evidence for the existence of gratuitous evils: 'a thin defence' rather than a 'thick defence' (Tracy 2007, 157-160). Murray's defences are composite — combinations of what Murray refers to as forms of *causa dei* (CD) : arguments in defence of God, the hope/intention being that the combination of defences offered will be enough to persuade the objector as well as encouraging the believer. It is the case that the success of any defence of the problem of evil is dependent on an individual's 'warranted acceptances' or presuppositions. However, in a combination of defences there might be, at least, one 'on offer' that is acceptable to the protagonist. Chapter 7 of Murray's book is actually entitled 'Combining CDs'. It follows that Murray isn't convinced that any (one) explanation for God's allowance of the existence of gratuitous evils is sufficient but that, taken together, some might suffice.

Murray takes an interesting excursion into the principle of Nomic Regularity i.e. the notion of 'chaos to order' through which God was able to bring forth a positive end product; the idea being that, at least partly, this Nomic Regularity (NR), is a sufficient reason for the 'developmental' necessity for animal suffering. In other words NR (in the universe) allowed for the actual evolution of biological life-forms and that this 'lengthy' process (with all the implications for suffering and death of numerous creatures) brought about the 'greater good' of creatures such as Homo Sapien Sapiens. Murray's NR is an essential feature of theistic evolution as it offers a 'signpost' for the existence of God. However, with regards to animal pain and suffering Murray states that, "...if justifiable at all, [it] is justified as a necessary condition for outweighing goods which either are enjoyed by creatures other than those that suffer or serve to enhance the goodness of the

God, Evolution, and Evil's Mystery

Julian Fernandes

universe at the global level." **(130)** Murray's question **(146)** as to whether or not there could have been a better world introduces a comment from the eccentrically brilliant Woody Allen, who suggested that the worst that could be said on God's behalf is that 'he's an under achiever'. Murray himself **(151-152)** states that a complete *causa dei* of this (NR) sort faces two 'insurmountable hurdles'. The first hurdle is that such an account does not seem to have the resources to explain why exactly there has to be so much pre-human animal pain and suffering, and secondly, that it is hard to see how the 'good' of free and effective choice by creatures like ourselves requires the existence of animals pre-existent to humans that have [to have] 'second-order mental states of the sort that make animal pain and suffering morally salient'. Murray's 'hurdle' is indeed difficult to assail unless the evolutionary path should have had no other means of bringing about *the unswerving plans* of the God who is there, and who cares deeply for all that he has made. However, the issue raised here is that of morality —God's morality—the perceived issue of 'natural evil'. Murray concludes **(164)** that the theist has good reason to believe that Nomic Regularity is 'a highly desirable feature of creation' and that it does explain a variety of types of natural evil, but that the theist would not have sufficient reason to think that animal suffering would be among them. Of course, apart from this nomic regularity there may never have arisen any prospect of the emergence (however temporal) of the abundant life that has appeared, over time, on this planet. NR aside— because 'higher-order-thought' creatures share the same vulnerability there might be sufficient reasons for this state of affairs—as Southgate **(2008, 16)** points out when he says that this world is the only possible type of world for such creatures to arise. We return to this notion in the final section of this thesis.

Murray (141) refers to George Frederick Wright who argued that intellectual goods were as significant as moral goods and that NR served the aims of both. Murray: "Indeed, for Wright, these intellectual pleasures were sufficiently good that they offset the natural evils that might occur as by-products of the nomic regularity of nature." (142) Of course, just because the world tends to follow rules or principles that produce an orderly system, it does not follow that the predictability of the ordered system (our world) is the kind of system an omniscient, omnipotent and benevolent mind would have engineered. It may, of course, indicate the existence of an intelligent cause but that may be all it does. To argue that the existence of suffering is the result of the activity of a system that functions in a regular way is fine but it tells us nothing whatsoever of the 'deity' behind such symmetry. The use of the NR may open the closed mind to the existence of God but, most likely, not to the goodness of God—in the face of the 'ills of evolution'. Murray though 'spreads the net'—hoping that his (or another's) CD is able to add weight to the general work of theodicy. Murray is aware of the extent of the problem in constructing such a defence. He writes: "Indeed, it seems quite implausible to think that an evil as widespread as the evil in question here, animal pain and suffering, could or would be explained only by appeal to one narrow range of goods that God aims to bring about through creation, and that certain types of permitted evil take such explanations seriatim." (195)

4.4   'The Groaning of Creation'

In the introduction of his book 'The Groaning of Creation' : God, Evolution and the Problem of Evil 2008', Christopher Southgate states (2) that species as we know them are as they are because of the pressure of natural selection and predator-prey cycles—and that, 'we can now see why pain and violence are

God, Evolution, and Evil's Mystery
Julian Fernandes

endemic in nature.' Southgate refers to the environmental philosopher and theologian Holmes Rolston III. Rolston, who having listed the more positive aspects of the evolutionary process, stated that, "... It is also, orderly, prolific, efficient, selecting for adaptive fit, exuberant, complex, diverse, regenerating life generation after generation." (3)

Southgate makes it clear (28 -40) that, in the light of biological evolution, the Adamic Fall account (*as the sole reason for the existence of physical death in nature*) is untenable on chronological grounds. Southgate's view of the tenability of the Adamic Fall, in the light of biological evolution, is important. However, even if the Adamic fall has no relevance for an evolutionary defence, it does not, necessarily, mean that the Adamic Fall is not of theological/actual significance. If, as Southgate suggests (8), death is actually a 'thermodynamic necessity', it is, indeed, difficult to imagine the biological process/system without death. We may well be dealing with a God who had but the one 'option' for his creation purposes. Southgate states (30) that even though we can never be sure that the evolutionary process was God's only way to give rise to creatures such as stem from the 3.8 or so billion-year-long evolution of the Earth's biosphere, we can only say that, given what we know about creatures—especially what is known about the role of the evolutionary process in refining biological characteristics, and the sheer length of time the process has required to give rise to sophisticated sentience—it is eminently plausible and coherent to suppose that this was the only way open to God[19].

---

[19] Southgate's is a good argument as the point is that it is God's use of evolution that is in question and it is the evolutionary process that is broadly accepted. The only thing here though is that it may be seen to diminish God's omnipotence—but does it? Not if we are referring to the 'received wisdom' that supports entirely the evolutionary package—with some 'emergent' qualification.

God, Evolution, and Evil's Mystery

Julian Fernandes

The 'Only Way' option is a view also held by, among others, R.J.Russell. Russell (2007, 109-151) gives detailed reasons for holding a view that is committed to biological evolution being the only way God could have produced the present day results. Should God have had only the 'one option' through which to create a world, one could, rightfully suppose that we are not dealing with an omnipotent God. Southgate, however, is not suggesting that the Triune God is anything other than omnipotent; however, it does follow that this aspect of God's 'being' might well be in question should it be that, somehow, the God of Christian belief could not have produced a better process for the achievement of the objectives of an omnipotent and omniscient God.

Southgate (pages 57-59) explores the notion of kenosis and its relevance for evolutionary theodicy and refers to the term 'deep intratrinitarian kenosis'—that the 'self-abandoning love of the Father in begetting the Son establishes an otherness that enables God's creatures to be (what Southgate terms) 'selves'. It is, therefore, 'selving'—the self-development of biological (sentient) 'selves'—the 'selving' goal of the evolutionary process that is seen by theists as a major goal of evolution. Should there have been no such thing as evolutionary process, there would, of course, have been no possibility for any such selving to occur. Southgate proposes that the evolutionary struggle of creation, 'can be read as being the "travail" to which God subjected creation *in hope* that the values of complex life, and ultimately freely choosing creatures such as ourselves, would emerge.' (95) It is, of course, a possibility that unguided [Darwinian] processes would produce less than the 'hoped-for' outcomes.

God, Evolution, and Evil's Mystery

Julian Fernandes

Southgate reminds his readers that he is not advancing the view that the evolutionary process has been damaged by 'Adamic' fallenness. Indeed, Southgate, as with most Christian evolutionists, realises the evident contradictions between a creation that is 'frustrated' and that 'groans (Romans 8:20-22) and a 'creation' that is the craftsmanship of a loving, caring, benevolent God. Indeed, this earthly state of affairs may be seen as a system that is in need of healing. Southgate maintains that we shall fulfil our co-redeeming role by becoming partners with God in the healing of our little corner of the cosmos, when we reveal our true Christ-likeness by having our minds set on servanthood. Moreover, we shall transcend ourselves not by the consummation of all our desires but through re-educating them with wisdom, so as to liberate the nonhuman creation from this particular mark of its travail. It is Southgate's contention that this renewing of the mind' (Romans 12:2) produces the necessary 'self-giving'—a self-giving (love) that emanates from the relationship within the Trinity. However, it is the human animal, rather than any other species, that fares best out of the evolutionary environment. Southgate, indeed, highlights the fact that the human animal has access to an extent of freedom and self-transcendence that goes vastly beyond what is present to other animals. However, we would suggest that 'potentiality' is not an absolute—mankind has the potential for both good and evil. Indeed, mankind may be, through the evolutionary process, [becoming] something 'ignoble' rather than something 'noble'; bearing the *Imago Dei* does not guarantee righteous choices, as both the Scriptures and the evidence of history confirm. Of course, for those in Christ the potential to bring about change is, indeed, enormous; but this is, for the present and future, a potentiality to be realised.

God, Evolution, and Evil's Mystery
Julian Fernandes

Whatever it is that God intends for humanity or other creatures at some point in the future, the facts are that the death of all creatures fuels evolutionary processes leading to the demise of the weak and the survival of the better equipped predator. Yet in spite of predation—before the appearance of modern-man—there would have existed a prolific, 'self-sustaining', abundant, diverse, creation. Death though can be seen as the final victor unless, somehow, God redeems the 'unfairness' and brings about whatever can be believed to be 'greater goods' for the recipients of the unjust treatment meted out by the evolutionary process. Indeed, Southgate (81) argues that a scientifically informed eschatology 'must' try and give some sort of account of what might be continuities and discontinuities between this creation and the new one. Any such future hope though does not depend on our present understanding of just how this universe (any parallel universes) or how any new planetary systems function, but on what God has promised in Scripture.

> Vital to this present project is my conviction that scientifically informed eschatology must also *try and relate* the great final transforming act of God, of which the resurrection of Christ is usually regarded as the beginning, not just to continuities and discontinuities in *human* life but also to our understanding of God's relation to living creatures other than human beings. (Southgate, 81-82)

Southgate, along with Murray, offers an amalgam of defences—the core of which (listed a-f) are as follows:

That the goodness of creation gives rise of all sorts of values:

a. That pain, suffering, death, and extinction are intrinsic to a creation evolving according to Darwinian principles.

b. That an evolving creation was the only way God could produce all the 'beauty, diversity, sentience, and sophistication that the biosphere exhibits.

c. That God co-suffers with every sentient being in creation.

d. That the Cross of Christ is 'the epitome' of divine compassion, God's assuming of ultimate responsibility for the pain of creation—the Cross inaugurating the transformation of creation (the ending of the groaning Paul refers to in Romans 8:22)

e. The importance of giving an account of how a loving God of loving relationship must provide an eschatological fulfillment for creatures that have no flourishing in this life—that such a God could never regard such a creature as 'a mere evolutionary expedient'.

f. If divine fellowship with creatures such as us is in any sense a goal of evolutionary creation—that this may lead to the possibility that humans have a crucial and positive role, cooperating with their God in the healing of the evolutionary process—the 'co-redeemer' argument. (16)[20]

That creation engenders many sorts of values is, without doubt, the case. Moreover, that an evolving creation was necessary for God's purposes is accepted as a 'given' in the majority of theistic evolutionary circles—a de facto, even

---

[20] Evolution though is, from the position of the argument in this thesis, not something that is broken—rather it is this way for a reason—and God has subjected the creation to this system so that God, in Christ, could redeem and transform it. Indeed, this is the only means through which God could resolve the problem of moral evil and to release the creation from its bondage

necessary, state of affairs. Southgate's argument that God co-suffers with every sentient being is plausible, as this would be a necessary expression of the compassion of the God of the Bible. However, we suggest that God as 'co-sufferer' does not indicate a culpability on God's part but rather speaks of an empathetic solidarity of God with his creatures.

It is agreed that some kind of 'eschatological fulfillment' for creatures that have 'no flourishing in this life' shall (somehow) pertain—though we have no idea how this would pertain. It is so hard for us to imagine a world without entropic consequences. Southgate's , view—that humans have a positive, cooperative role with God in the healing of the evolutionary process, is interesting. However, considering the late arrival of '**the**' species with both the means (*technologically & politically*) and the will (*morally & ethically*) to address the prevailing state of affairs, Southgate's suggestion cannot be of major significance. However, it could be argued that this was God's intention regarding the people of Israel (C. Wright 2006) and that it continues to be God's intention regarding those professing to follow Christ in the 'latter days'.

4.5 A Barthian theodicy of nature

Evolutionary theory has exacerbated the problem of natural evil for the believer—leaving the existence of benevolence within the character of the Godhead questionable. Darwinian Natural Selection has, without doubt, greatly diminished the likelihood of there being a satisfactory outcome in the work of theodicy. Neil Messer, however, offers a possible way ahead.

At the beginning of his chapter in the edited book *Theology after Darwin*, Messer (2009, 139) outlines his intended course—stating that a more satisfactory

God, Evolution, and Evil's Mystery
Julian Fernandes

approach to the problem of evolutionary evil is to be taken from the perspective of Christian tradition rather than from any scientific interpretation or overview. Messer also refers to his own approach and that it is developed in dialogue with the twentieth century Swiss theologian Karl Barth. Messer refers to 'Mapping the Problem of Evolutionary Evil'—making reference to two strands: the stronger strand advocating that the evolutionary process is the means that God used to 'create' all biological life. *The weaker claim* is that which applies to...the conviction that the world which God made and pronounced 'very good' (Genesis 1:31) is a world that has a process of evolution by natural selection built into it'. (140) Messer suggests that one obstacle that modern biology 'seems' to place in the way of both the weak and strong claims is that the evolutionary process inevitably entails 'ills' or 'evils' i.e. the pain and death of all creatures. It is this 'inevitability' factor that poses the problem—markedly within the world of evolutionary theodicy.

Messer offers an alternative approach to the problem and refers to two aspects of approaches to the problem of evil. Firstly he refers to the apparent contradiction between the world disclosed to us by evolutionary biology and the creation that God (Genesis 1:31) pronounces 'very good'. Secondly, he refers to the more familiar question of whether an omnipotent God could have avoided some of the evil that we find in the world. Regarding the latter Messer states that there is a danger that if Christians pursue this line of thought too far, 'they will find themselves defending an idol of their own making rather than the God of Christian revelation.' (147). This is taken to mean that taking such a route often leads to dead-ends or an adventure in metaphysical gymnastics rather than an adequate theodicy. Messer's point, as viewed here, is that any 'enquiry' of this sort needs to start with the Christian community's confession of faith in response to the biblical witness. Messer is fully aware of the problems and lists the major difficulties:

a. That the Scriptures witness to a God who created all that is, and who pronounced the creation 'very good' (Genesis 1:31).

b. That the Genesis creation narratives and other biblical texts flesh out what we are to understand by 'very good',' a world of peace and plenty.' Messer states that if, in any sense, the Christian doctrine of creation and Darwinian evolutionary biology are referring to the same world, then we seem to be faced with a contradiction. (148)

The 'contradiction' Messer refers to in 'b' is that the God of the Bible would not have devised such a system as the one in question and then declared it 'very good'. Here we disagree with Messer and uphold that, in spite of what Messer feels to be a contradiction, it is possible to affirm—along with Scripture: that creation was 'very good', in the sense of being fit for purpose[21]. Southgate's response (2011) to this is that Messer is, "...simply unwilling to concede that the disvalues we see in evolution could be part of God's creation." (14). Southgate suggests that it seems that in order to retain belief in 'the unequivocal goodness of God's creation', Messer wants to draw instead on Barth's 'Church Dogmatics' in which Barth reflects on this concept of 'nothingness'.

---

[21] Or as Polkinghorne (1991) suggests: it was good because it had 'fruitful potentiality'. The view held here, though, is that any notion of 'potentiality' must take into consideration God's sovereign purposes—the purposes of a God who has the wherewithal to bring about an ultimate telos—this being in stark contrast to a God who has no means of bringing about His plans and purposes.

God, Evolution, and Evil's Mystery

Julian Fernandes

Regarding 'beginnings', Messer follows Barth, Southgate (2008, 5) and others when he states that there never was a 'golden age'—never an idyllic period on earth when there was no predation, parasitism or plague. 'The first man was immediately the first sinner'[Barth,1956]. According to Messer, Barth is saying that history begins with the Fall—that the history of the world has always been a 'fallen history' (149). However, this does not mean that the story of creation can be contradicted by the [so] different history supplied by evolutionary biology. Messer points out that Barth is not attempting an explanation of the origins of evil but that Barth is more interested in what God has done about the problem. This is all very well but it seems to rather 'muddy the waters' . 'Barth', Messer states, identifies evil as 'nothingness' (*das Nichtige*). As such 'nothingness' has a strange, paradoxical, negative kind of existence: it is the chaos, disorder and annihilation that threatens God's creation—a threat to which God is opposed. Sin is one form that 'nothingness' takes, but it also takes the forms of suffering and death. Furthermore, it is clear that not only humanity, but the whole of God's creation is threatened and opposed by this 'nothingness': "Whatever in the evolutionary process is opposed to God's creative purpose is to be identified with 'nothingness': it is an aspect of the chaos and disorder threatening the creation." (149) [22] [23]

---

[22] Barth's use of the term 'nothingness' seems to be less than satisfactory—especially if this 'nothingness' is to be defeated by 'something'. Whether or not it avoids the problem of dualism is debatable.

[23] Walter Brueggemann (2009) refers to the hymnic tradition of Israel being, "...surely aware of the old and pervasive mythos of primordial combat, exuberantly announces that YHWH has defeated and dispelled the forces of evil...that YHYH is indeed the Creator of all the 'hosts', the powers of heaven and their work at YHWH's command..." (Brueggemann 2009, 147). That there was 'a personified' opposition to God's creative purposes rather than any abstract nothingness, is an essential part of the argument in this thesis as shall become apparent in the latter sections.

God, Evolution, and Evil's Mystery
Julian Fernandes

Messer affirms that the Biblical witness requires us to say of the world: that it is both created and fallen, that creation is the work of God, that it was pronounced 'very good', and that it is badly astray from what God means it to be[24]. In contradistinction to Messer's view, the view held here is that creation, in terms of God's planned intentions is (though it is impossible to qualify because of the unverifiable effects of the behaviour of fallen angels) as God intended—that creation has an evolutionary 'blueprint' because of the planned intentions of the God who is both benevolent and sovereign[25]. Messer (150) aligns himself with an evolutionary perspective and states that it is the evolutionary process that has made us the way we are. However, he follows Barth in identifying the violence and scarcity of the struggle for existence with what he considers 'the fallenness of the world'. The argument in this thesis though is that there is, indeed, a fallenness but that the cause of that fallenness need not remain unexamined—an 'unknown cause' or an 'abstract form'—a *das Nichtige* that leaves aside the need for an answer to the problem of evil—but rather that the fallenness, of angels and of men—though **_not_** instigated by God was, somehow, known by God before the creation of the universe. For this world is the best possible world in which the Triune God brings about the best of possible outcomes.

Messer **is** concerned not to blur the edges—'making God's good creative purpose and the flawed evolutionary process into two co-eternal powers vying for the

---

[24] It's interesting to note that Messer (2009, 150) thinks that there could be closer links than we sometimes think between the violence of the struggle for existence and—at least some aspects of human sin. We agree with this—it is so much more than we see or even perceive.

[25] This is not to say that created agents have not brought about states of affairs that may be considered a contradiction , regarding God's attributes of benevolence and sovereignty, but that are nothing of the sort.

upper hand in shaping us.' Neither is Messer wishing to re-invent a form of Manichaeism, in which light battles darkness or any form of Gnosticism[26]—where the material world is irretrievably flawed and salvation lies in escaping from it. The reason we don't have to do either of these things, Messer suggests, is because God has, in Christ, addressed our predicament. According to Messer, Barth held that in the incarnation God exposed Himself to nothingness—doing so in order to repel and defeat it. Messer adds to this by referring to Paul's words in 1 Corinthians 15:3-4 where the apostle states that, "Christ died for our sins in accordance with the scriptures, and that he was buried, and that he was raised from the dead on the third day in accordance with the scriptures."

Messer affirms that, "Because this is the heart of the [Christian] good news, Gnosticism is not an option: the Christian gospel promises not an escape from the material but its healing and transformation...The Christian tradition understands the resurrection of Christ as the in-breaking of God's promised new age into history, the first fruits of what God promises to do to *make all things new'. Revelation 21:5* " (151) It is, as Messer suggests, the 'transformation' that is the good news. However, should there be any need of 'healing' the inference would be that the creation is out of sorts with its creator or that another party/parties had ruined the ideal. Messer admits that the kind of world to which—" ...a wolf hath sojourned with a lamb, And a leopard with a kid doth lie down, And calf, and young lion, and fatling are together, And a little youth is leader over them." (Isaiah 11:6-9[27]) is beyond our [present] comprehension *especially in the light of evolutionary biological outcomes.*

---

[26] Neither is this the view in the argument in this thesis—in which neither Dualism (Gnostic or otherwise) or any other proposed opposition to the sovereign will of God could obtain.

[27] Young's Literal Translation

However, because of his high view of biblical revelation and his insistence that theological interpretation take precedence over any scientifically derived *a priori*—this is Messer's position. Messer is correct in this—for it is the 'theological' that is in question and not, at present, the 'scientific'. Messer affirms what is the Christian hope: that God's peace, not the struggle for existence, will have the last word—and because God's '*good future*' has broken into our [present] with the resurrection of Christ, we are able to see the past and the beginning in a true light as well.

In the final part of his discourse (154) Messer admits that his 'picture' does not offer much by way of explanation—of how the struggle for existence came to be such a pervasive feature of our present reality. He does suggest, however, that the important question to report is what God has actually done to address our predicament and our response to God's solution. Messer's is a familiar voice. Reaching into the eschaton for consolation may well be preferable to wallowing in the [muddy] waters of the 'dim' past but this in and of itself does not match up to an adequate defence, let alone a theodicy. However, Messer's commitment to the prioritising of the revelation of God (in Scripture) over the, present, conclusions of mankind 'the latter-day fruit of evolution' is one readily concurred with. Indeed, it is because of the revelation of Scripture—declaring the omnipotence and benevolence of God—that the problem arises otherwise there is no such problem.

4.6   Against Instrumentalism: animals and the fall

Michael Lloyd (Are Animals Fallen? 1998), along with Neil Messer, realises that the problem of an evolutionary theodicy is acute for the Christian defender as it entails dealing with the contradictions of a world in which the 'love of God' is

God, Evolution, and Evil's Mystery
Julian Fernandes

[has not been] altogether evident and states that, "It is *certainly* not the sort of world which one would expect the God we meet in Christ to have created." (Lloyd 1998, 148) Moreover, Lloyd states that the protest against, what he refers to as, 'the predatory character of nature' is precisely because of the Christological conception of God held by Christians. It is though far broader than any underdeveloped Christology, for, it is the very idea of the 'Sovereign God' (The Triune God of Scripture) that **is** in question. In other words, the life and teachings of the incarnate son of God cannot be taken in isolation from the actual telos of the Triune God—a telos that has to do with justice as well as redemption—with judgement as well as reconciliation.

Regarding the defence offered by instrumentalists (that God will bring good out of harms and that the harms are a necessary part of the 'plot') Lloyd comments that, "...even without pain, predation does not seem unambiguously to declare the glory of God, and theodicies which seek to justify predation as part of the creational purposes of God tend to adopt anti-Christian attitudes in the attempt." (1998, 149) Lloyd points out that with an instrumentalist view of evolution God is "responsible for the suffering involved, but not culpable, because God is using it as an instrument in the pursuit of some greater good, be it aesthetic richness or human freedom." (151) Lloyd though says that 'Eschatology by itself is not sufficient however great the happiness, peace and rest on offer they do not justify the means, and that the problem must be addressed at the other end as well. Lloyd argues (155) that what is needed is an account of evil in which God is not only victoriously against it at the end but is also resolutely against it at the beginning. In other words, we need a doctrine of the Fall as well as an end times solution. We absolutely affirm Lloyd's view—*vis a vis* the need for a

comprehensive defence that takes into account all the necessary ingredients —
but come to a different conclusion on the matter.

Lloyd is convinced that the only possible defence for God against the charge of
making a world riddled with suffering and violence is that God didn't: "And that
is what the doctrine of the Fall tells us." (155) Lloyd's view sees the Fall as cosmic
and not local, and that it is not limited to human sin. Lloyd's view also sees that
animals are part of a fallen creation and therefore subject to its state of affairs. He
notes that those who hold to the fallenness of the whole of creation do so not
primarily to get faith out of an apologetic hole, but for intrinsic theological and
Christological reasons which they see embedded in the revelation of God in
Christ and Scripture. Lloyd though states that since the arrival of Darwinism the
effects of the human fall could no longer be taken as the cause of predation and
death and states that:

> The question must now be faced as to how that which was inimical to the
> creational intention of an omnipotent God could have come to be.
> Granted that the whole of creation is fallen, how did it fall? Granted that
> the divisions of creation are not a design fault of the Creator but the result
> of free decisions by free creatures, what account may we give of the
> volitional process or processes which brought about the Fall?" (156) [28]

---

[28] Lloyd refers to the work of the twentieth century theologian N.P.Williams (1998, 157-157) who
rejected the idea that humans were 'the ultimate culprits' for all of the ills within the evolutionary
scheme of things but, nevertheless, insisted that the Fall must have taken place in time as any
attempt to lift the ultimate origin of evil out of time would plunge us into the gulf of either
dualism or of unmoral monism.

Lloyd himself prefers to work with a model of the Fall as angelic in origin. He suggests that the hypothetical assertion that natural evil is the result of the distortion of creation brought about by the angelic fall does not need evidential support at this precise point if it can be shown that it is organically related to a world-view which is coherent and carries evidential support at other key points[29], "...the doctrine of the Fall implies that creation is fallen, that it does not reflect the self-giving love of God that we meet in Christ, and that the God we do meet in Christ is the sort of God who gives creatures that freedom to reject God's purposes without which love is meaningless. If we understand 'godless' to mean 'having turned away from God',..." (160) Indeed, the expressive free will of both angels and men are at the root of the problem of moral evil—the effects of which are, as yet, not fully comprehended. As Lloyd has stated, and as is agreed with here; Free Will is a necessary part of the outworking of God's creative purposes. If this is the case then there must be some cause and effect resulting from free will decisions. However, as Southgate points out, "...a position such as Lloyd's still suffers from the problem...that it dissects out the biological world and assigns all the disvalue to the free (harmful) choices of angels, and all the values to God's creative work." (2011, 235) Southgate is correct in his assessment of Lloyd's (1998) work but this is not the final word on the viability of a Free-Will defence per se—as will become evident in part two of this thesis.

4.7 Two Theodicies: Irenaeus & Augustine, as interpreted by R.J. Russell

---

[29] Lloyd refers to past theories related to the existence of objects in the universe that were later proven to be factual. A current example might be the Higgs Boson. We address the notion of an Angelic Fall in part two of this thesis.

God, Evolution, and Evil's Mystery
Julian Fernandes

Robert J. Russell (2008) has done much to set out a conceptual framework for considering the problem of evolutionary theodicy. Russell draws heavily from the work of Irenaeus as he develops his defence of the goodness of God in the light of evolution.Russell proposes that any 'robust theodicy' has to meet at least three criteria:

a) it must ward off Manichean tendencies to "blame God" for creating natural evil or to view nature as unambiguously evil,

b) it must ward off Pelagian tendencies to undercut the universality of moral evil,

c) it must fully take on board [Darwinian] evolution, and in particular the constitutive character of natural evil to life. (255)

Russell notes that Christian theology includes a variety of theodicies (defences) that meet these criteria, and refers to John Hick's analysis of this variety as falling into two broad types—the Augustinian and Irenaean; Russell then endeavours to reformulate these theodicies so that they meet all three criteria—deploying them to the task of evolutionary theodicy. Russell offers some cautionary comments and interesting insights regarding Augustine's 'Free Will Defence' and suggests that, for Augustine, both natural and moral evils are 'ultimately' the result of the actions of free rational beings who sin. According to Russell, Augustine's view was that sin began with the cosmic fall of the angels and continued with Adam and Eve who, though created 'very good' by God, did of their own free will choose creaturely goods over God. (255)

1. Extending the Augustinian Theodicy to Physics and Cosmology

Russell suggests that there are resources in Augustinian theodicy which should not be overlooked (257) and refers to the work of Reinhold Niebuhr who suggested that the first task required—in order to divest the Augustinian theodicy of its 'creation/fall' framework—was to uncover its underlying philosophical argument and then to reinterpret this argument in an evolutionary perspective:

> Niebuhr then rendered the underlying logic of the Augustinian theodicy as asserting that sin is *unnecessary but inevitable*. This phrase captures Augustine's argument without tying it to the Fall[30]. It expresses in stark terms what Niebuhr called the 'absurd paradox' of the Christian free-will defence. Augustinian theodicy rephrased through Niebuhr's formation now meets our three criteria for an evolutionary theodicy. (257)

Under the heading: '*Preconditions in physics that underlie the free-will defence*' Russell asks, what, in particular, must physics be like for the reformulated Augustinian /Niebuhrian free-will defence to hold. Moreover, what, if anything, reflects the Niebuhrian logic of 'unnecessary but inevitable' at the level of physics? Russell refers to thermodynamics—and the work of what he terms 'metaphorical theology' summarising the views of its exponents thus:

> To summarise the idea briefly, we typically find beauty and goodness in the patterns of emergent complexity and creative novelty characteristic of life, while tragedy and sorrow play themselves out in terms of the dissipation and destruction associated with decay, disease and death. Curiously, thermodynamics underlies and is entailed by all these phenomena. The second law [of thermodynamics] thus plays a *dual* role: It

---

[30] This, as shall be argued in part two of this thesis, is a mistake as it does not take into consideration the potential for both good and evil that God has allowed within the created order—so does not allow for a more comprehensive free-will argument.

makes possible the physical and biological consequences of our moral action both for good and for ill. (258)

The unavoidable conclusion of Niebuhrian logic seems to be that sin (deviant behaviour, disobedience etc.) is the de facto result of the system through which God has created life-forms—including sentient beings such as 'Adam and Eve'. The question becomes, as Russell underlines: "Why did God choose to create this universe with these laws of physics knowing that they would not only make Darwinian evolution unavoidable, and with it the sweep of natural evil in the biological realm, but that they would also contribute to natural evil at the level of physics...." (Russell, 259) Russell's conclusion on the matter is that the 'Augustinain/Niebuhrian theodicy (ultimately) fails. So, why does it fail? It fails, according to Russell, not because it is tied to a 'mythical fall',because it is not. Neither is its failure due to it mistaking death as a consequence of 'sin' and not as constitutive of life. It avoids both admirably. According to Russell, it leads to the (unhelpful) recognition that , 'underlying moral evil is natural evil' and that this recognition (conclusion) characterises the universe as a whole.
Evil is intrinsic to the processes that generate value.[31] Russell, therefore, looks to the redemption of the cosmos.

---

[31] We agree with Russell here—that evil is moral rather than natural. Moreover, it is the case that if the laws of physics functioned to different values there might well be no likelihood of the entropic effects of the Second Law of Thermodynamics; thus, in such a world, there may not be the physical means through which the results of rebellious malevolence could manifest itself. Natural evil, paradoxically, exists as a result of moral deviancy but, as we shall argue in the conclusion of this thesis—this is the only possible world in which the second person of the Trinity could take on flesh, suffer and die—in so doing rescue, ransom and redeem a creation that 'groans'—in the waiting.

2. <u>Extending Schleiermacher's Theodicy to Evolution</u>

Russell then returns to the work of John Hick—'retrieving and extending' his ideas. Russell (260) comments on what he refers to as Hick's helpful comparison of both contrasts and agreements between the theodicies of Augustine and Schleiermacher (the latter deriving some of its inspiration from Irenaeus). The essence of the difference between these theodicies, according to Russell's interpretation of Hick's views, is as follows:

- o The Augustinian theodicy looks at a created paradise in the past and focuses crucial importance on the fall of angels and humankind—looking to a future of judgement for 'the damned'.
- o The Irenaean theodicy accepts evil as an inevitable factor in the world— suited for moral development. It does not deny the Fall, but rejects the ideas of 'lost righteousness and inherited sinfulness'. It views an eternal hell as 'rendering a Christian theodicy impossible'. (260)

Russell states that the key difference, as he reads Hick, is that the Augustinian theodicy attempts to protect God from responsibility for the existence of evil by stressing the Fall (Adamic & Angelic), whereas the Irenaean theodicy accepts God's ultimate responsibility for evil while 'showing' why a world that includes evil can be considered justifiable and inevitable.

> For the Augustinian theodicy the world is 'very good' as it is now, even including the reality of sin and evil. For the Irenaean theodicy the perfection of the world lies in the eschatological future where the end, the Kingdom of God, will justify the means of its achievement...The

> Augustinian theodicy admits that bringing good out of evil is better than not permitting evil to exist...Irenaean theodicy treats it as central and stresses the eschatological context of the 'greater good'. (261)

Russell's (2008) conclusion: that *'the end is a means to the beginnings'*—that God will bring an ideal end-times solution—that all will be well so there is no need to search for an elusive answer for the state of affairs seems less than satisfactory. His explanation for the state of affairs within the created order seems to be reasonably plausible but at the same time it does not seem to offer a complete account of the extent of evil in the world. Moreover, in order to avoid any 'fall confusion' it tempts one to engage in an eschatological just-so story—and at the same time avoiding contact with the problem of evil per se.

The argument in this thesis sets out to offer a defence that agrees and encompasses much of what has been said previously—but that offers a different conclusion not previously advanced in the literature.

5. Precursory Chapter to the Proposed Model

In this chapter we interact particularly with the views of Stephen H. Webb as given in his book entitled 'The Dome of Eden: A New Solution to the Problem of Creation and Evolution'. Webb's views that evolution works under divine permission and that the emergence of Humankind has particular significance within an evolutionary paradigm have a particular symmetry with the argument in this thesis[32].

---

[32] Although Webb's view, that this world is NOT the best of possible worlds, is at odds with the argument given in part two of this thesis, Webb's views are nonetheless helpful regarding its development.

God, Evolution, and Evil's Mystery
Julian Fernandes

Webb notes that evolution leaves a trail in history—marked by blood and anguish. What Webb avoids saying here is that it is this very 'trail of blood and anguish' (made possible by the natural laws) that the Triune God 'commissioned' and ordained. It is however, as we shall argue in part two, this very state of affairs that allows for the victory of God over both sin and death. Indeed, the song the faithful will sing and the creation will echo is that of the Victory of God over sin and death; it will be a continual song declaring the gracious mercy and goodness of the Godhead[33]. It is this world (a world ordained and created by God) that is the only possible world in which the free will of conscious beings can pertain with all of the resultant consequences and, most importantly, the redemptive act of the crucified Son of God could possibly take place.

We concur with Webb's views (246-295) on the 'emergence' of human kind as being a significant 'event' in the evolution of carbon based life-form—conscious, intelligent, incredibly creative, morally aware and, most importantly, 'God conscious'. Webb's views coalesce with the argument given in this thesis—that God [incarnate], at the eschaton, would dwell with a redeemed creation having rescued and redeemed the creation from its bondage to corruption. Humankind, Webb argues, is meant to be here—moreover the emergence of humans has been a major part[34] of God's 'creation project'. Webb makes the point that: if God

---

[33] Donald Macleod (2000), referring to the work of B.B. Warfield says that the revelation of the trinity was made not in word but in deed: "It was made in the incarnation of God the Son, and the outpouring of God the Holy Spirit...the revelation of the Trinity was incidental to, and the inevitable effect of, the accomplishment of redemption." (154)

[34]Our argument does not devalue the rest of creation or suppose that God has little more than a utilitarian purpose for it. Robert. J. Russell advocates that the suffering of creatures cannot 'alone ' be justified by the evolution of Homo sapiens and their destiny with God: "Instead, the suffering

chose this world as the stage for the incarnation, and the human species as its form, then there must be something unique about both planet Earth and human nature. Indeed Webb argues that one of the corollaries of Christ's primacy is that humans have the form (and image) precisely because God intended to give a human form to Christ from the beginning. Webb states that the Old Testament has not only an anthropomorphic view of God but also a 'theomorphic' view of humanity, *i.e.* that humans take the form they do because God has the form he has—in Christ the Son. Webb makes it clear that sceptics will view his position as anthropomorphism (in the most negative of terms). He understands the reason for the critique well enough but points out that they are mistaken to claim that Christians think of everything from a human perspective and he suggests that God made the world with mankind in mind, to become friends of the Son and to accompany him in praise forever. (179)

Webb contends that theologians who argue that this world is the only world that God could have created run the risk, in their attempt to justify God's relationship with natural evil, of 'portraying' the world as thoroughly and necessarily evil, "That is, if there is no possible world that God could have created that would have been without evil, then the very existence of matter is thoroughly saturated in and inseparable from evil. If evil is built into nature, however, it is God who put it there." (96) Webb's point—that if evil is built into nature, it is God who put it there, clearly rules out the possibility of a third party being responsible for, at

---

of creatures is taken up *individually* by God in the incarnation, suffered by God in the crucifixion, and redeemed by God in the Resurrection. This eschatological act of God is to be seen as proleptically present to and with each creature at its death." (2012, 106) Russell may well be correct. This view may be considered speculative but it is nevertheless plausible. Indeed, the effects of the Cross of Christ need to be viewed in proleptic terms—as it is in Christ's life, death and resurrection that we have sight of the 'big picture'.

God, Evolution, and Evil's Mystery
Julian Fernandes

least, natural evil. Webb is correct in that God has allowed certain of his creatures the gift of choice and that, consequently, this 'gift' has allowed for the inflicting of an enormous amount of harms. <u>However</u>, this does not mean that God is guilty by default, rather that God has allowed for the kind of creation that is able to express itself. This, in our opinion, is a good outcome rather than a bad outcome. Webb makes a salient point though (97) when he says that evil (in the natural world) is real whereas entropy is exactly "what one would expect to find at the level of physical processes". Evil (Webb does not differentiate between natural and moral evil) is, from this perspective, a malevolent factor whereas entropy is, simply, the consequence of certain physical conditions. Webb however points out that even though the temptation to equate evolution with evil is understandable; equating nature with evil runs counter to the Christian tradition, most notably the claim found in Genesis that nature is good, which for Webb seems to mean 'moral' rather than 'utilitarian'. The view held here is that creation does not have the moral dimension that Webb may wish to assign to it. In this sense nature is amoral. Indeed, Webb reminds us that groups that considered nature evil (Manicheans and Cathars in particular) have always been considered heretical. He maintains (127) that any adequate theological account of evolution has to explain how God (as the source of all that is good in nature) bears no responsibility for evil evident within the evolutionary cycle of life. Webb here uses the term 'evil' but a more appropriate word would be 'harms'—as the results of [natural] entropy need not be considered 'evil' per se. The argument in this thesis is that neither God's universal laws nor the outcomes of these laws are 'naturally' evil, in and of themselves; they are nothing of the sort. That there are 'harmful outcomes' to these laws is a de facto given; that these outcomes are, most often, horrendous—even maliciously harmful to life's outcomes—is accepted. But this does not prove that this world is not the best possible world neither does it prove that the natural laws themselves are morally deficient. The outcomes of the effects of the natural laws on carbon-based-life may be reprehensible (from our perspective) but that is all that they can be[35]. Webb's view is that entropy is what one would expect to find at the level of physical processes (as referred to earlier) whereas 'evil' is something other than 'evil'; this obviously demands an explanation. For Webb the answer to the problem of evil has to be located outside of the evolutionary paradigm rather than within. This is, indeed, a sentiment concurred with in this thesis—particularly with regard to the 'labelling of nature as evil'. However, the conclusions in this thesis are somewhat different than Webb's. Webb's 'theses' (139-180) though are relevant to the argument in this thesis, as they helpfully open up a vista that offers some clarity regarding the rebellion of Satan and the angels:

i) Satan's Fall is a 'fall from grace' and is not to be confused with a 'fall from heaven to earth'. The argument here is that Satan's 'fall from grace' should be considered a *pre-creation-of-the-physical-universe event*. In other words outside of the space/time continuum. Whereas Satan's being cast down to the earth was, obviously, not. Satan was cast down into the world we know—an existent world of predation and death.

ii) Eden was a real place though not real in the sense that we can plot its coordinates on the space-time-continuum that we experience today.

---

[35] It may be acceptable to bring judgement against God with insufficient evidence. This is common practice—as C.S. Lewis points out, God is guilty—as 'proven'. "He (man) is the judge: God is in the dock. He (man) is quite a kindly judge: if God should have a reasonable defence for being the God who permits…The trial may even end in God's acquittal. But the important thing is that man is on the Bench and God in the Dock." (Lewis, 93)

God, Evolution, and Evil's Mystery

Julian Fernandes

If Eden is a real place, and if Satan tries to battle God in nature from some point in the space-time-continuum then there has to be some kind of 'reality' that divides Eden from the rest of the world. The effects of moral deviancy had to cross into Eden in order to disrupt it and to corrupt it—as Scripture indicates. The 'evil' that Webb refers to is that which can be described as 'moral' rather than 'natural'. This evil comes about as the result of the deviant behaviour of advanced created intelligence: extra-terrestrial and terrestrial alike. The outcomes of this evil, though affecting/infecting certain aspects of the created order, do not bring about major changes to the laws that God had ordained for his creation ordinances—the laws that enable the evolutionary process.

iii) That the reason for Satan's fall to come full circle is the same reason for creation as a whole, and is the reason why human nature cannot be reduced to its biological components: God created the world because God the Father had already determined to take the form of God the Son, and the form God the Father gave to the son is the same form in which mankind was created.

The world and all that is in it is a gift to the Son from the Father. If something like the human species, with its intelligence, its eyes and who knows what of other parts and features, is inevitable, then biology must have been conditioned from the very beginning to unfold the human pattern. That is exactly what the Primacy of Christ leads us to expect. Indeed the Primacy of Christ can be considered the metaphysical precondition made necessary by the phenomenon of evolutionary convergences. (Webb 2010, 267)

God, Evolution, and Evil's Mystery

Julian Fernandes

Robert C. Doyle (1999) argues that it is clear from the contents of Genesis chapters 1 to 3, as well as the way Scripture uses these chapters, that the basis for any understanding of the last things is in the understanding of the first things. Doyle's observation is that the beginning of the Bible—the beginning of time, the world, humankind, and humankind's relationship to God and the world—is pregnant with purpose. The purpose, the end (the eschaton) is implicit in the beginning (26) Regarding the six days of creation Doyle proposes that these six days actually find their significance in the seventh, "...the divine rest on the seventh day indicates the goal of creation." (26) This, we, along with Doyle maintain is a goal which shall be maintained, "...despite any rebellious efforts to vitiate it." (26) The argument in this thesis offers the same reasoning as Doyle's summary, i.e. that God's plan for the creation is purposeful, that it incorporates the alpha and 'the' omega with the telos of creation being finally revealed at the eschaton.

Throughout this thesis, we have argued that the creation is good—good in terms of it being good and not evil. We have maintained that the creation is as it is because its evolutionary process has been a necessary state of affairs rather than the product of an amorphous deity or of [mere] elemental forces. We have said that creation's evolution coalesces with the purposes (telos) of a God who is personal—a determinate entity rather than a force that defies description—sitting more comfortably with current trends in philosophical theology. We have further argued that God (The God of Scripture) is both sovereign and benevolent. Moreover we have said that, rather than being the product of a deficient deity or a defiant adversary, the creation is as it is because its evolution has been a necessary state of affairs and that, though considered less than satisfactory by created beings, is indeed a necessary state of affairs, and that (at the eschaton)

God, Evolution, and Evil's Mystery
Julian Fernandes

God will bring deliverance for those longing, as the apostle Paul intimates in his letter to the Christians in Rome, "...for the revealing of the sons of God." (Romans 8:19)

Part Two

An Eight Step Defence

The 'eight step' defence offered here follows the following order:

1. That it is a good for God to create a world containing beauty, diversity and complexity of creatures.
2. That such a world can only arise via an evolutionary process, which also necessitates suffering and apparent waste.
3. That only such a world is capable of being transformed into the 'new creation', in which there need be no more suffering.
4. But also, there is evidence that angels exist.
5. That Angels may have existed before the creation of this universe.
6. That it is a good that God gave angels freedom.
7. That angels rebelled and continued to oppose God's will for humans and the rest of creation.
8. That only such a world as this could make possible the incarnation of the divine Son and thereby the defeat of the angels through the power of the Cross.

God, Evolution, and Evil's Mystery
Julian Fernandes

Step 1. It is good for God to create a world containing beauty, diversity and complexity of creatures:

It is a most likely state of affairs that—should the God of the Bible desire to create a world—it would contain: beauty, diversity and a complexity of creatures. This is such a world.

> O LORD, how manifold are your works!
> In wisdom have you made them all;
> the earth is full of your creatures.
>
> (Psalm 104:1)

James L.Grenshaw suggests that the author of Psalm 104 looks beyond the tiny space occupied by humans, "His sweeping survey extends to all creatures and, more importantly, to their creator. Indeed, his sole point of mentioning a variety of animals and their thumb-endowed rival is to laud divine benevolence and wisdom." (2005, 5) Grenshaw adds, "...although the psalmist acknowledges the predatory action of lions during the night, the consequence of this behaviour is construed as a divine gift." (5) In this sense it can be said that, whatever the purpose of the living organism and whatever the 'life-experience' of any such creature, its creation is a good thing—even regarding some of the less positive life-forms that were in existence 'a while' before the arrival of the 'interpreters' of the evolution of biological life.

Regarding the 'Chance & Necessity' of the evolutionary process, John Polkinghorne (1986, 51) says, "... without chance there would be no change and development and without necessity there would be no preservation and selection." In his later work entitled 'The God of Hope and End of the World

(2002) Polkinghorne states that, "...through the intricate unfolding of physical processes initial simplicity has generated immense complexity... Theologically one can understand this complexity as the result of creation's having been endowed by its creator with a profound potentiality which has been allowed to explore and realise as it makes itself." (2002, 15) Polkinghorne's position is one that envisages an evolutionary-creation scenario in which God does not 'control' all of creation (as would a 'tyrannical puppeteer') but rather one of a creator whose, "...nature of love is patient and subtle, content to achieve the divine purposes in an open and developing way, in which the creatures themselves collaborate." (Polkinghorne, 15)

Whatever one may conclude regarding the above view of the **_actual_** level of God's interaction with the physical world; it is this world that allows for such diversity and complexity. It is, however, good for God to have created such potentiality—such complexity, diversity and beauty. David Wilkinson (2009) states that we need firstly to take seriously the notion that the heavens declare the glory of God (Psalm 19:1)—and that, "God may choose to reveal himself through the natural world, the book of his works as well as through the book of his word." (21) In referring to the cosmic picture of Christ, Wilkinson states that, "...this cosmic picture of Jesus suggests that God is the sustainer of order in creation. Paul in Colossians 1:17 reminds us that Christ is before all things , but also that 'in him all things hold together'[36]. This is a very different picture from the deistic Creator who lights the blue touch paper of the Big Bang and then goes

---

[36] We take it that in this passage the apostle is referring to the 'pre-existence' of Christ and to the 'supremacy' of Christ—that a straight forward exegesis of the passage does not render any notion of panentheism.

off to have a cup of tea. The verb is in the perfect indicating everything held together in him and continues to do so." (Wilkinson 2009, 24)

The heavens, indeed, declare the glory of God. Scripture enunciates the unseen glory that is being revealed in the creation—that God both creates and sustains; that there is an overall 'goodness' about the Creation—that the absolute goodness of the creation will be finally revealed at the eschaton.[37]

In referring to the progress, complexity and diversity of life, Simon Conway Morris (2003) states that, "…when within the animals we see the emergence of larger and more complex brains, sophisticated vocalizations, echolocation, electrical perception, advanced social systems including eusociality, viviparity, warm-bloodedness, and agriculture—all of which are convergent—then to me that sounds like progress." (307) Conway Morris' description paints a picture of an abundantly creative process that may be described as good. Ergo, it is good that God should have so done. Moreover, it is most unlikely that such an abundant array of life could have been produced by any other means or by any other deity—'tyrannical puppeteer' or otherwise.John Haught (2010, 69) says that, "…the fact that natural selection produces design, diversity, and what Darwin calls the 'descent of man' does not exclude the possibility that the evolutionary drama carries a hidden meaning and that it is directional in a very profound sense because it bears invisibly within it the cooperative influence of a liberating and promising God." It is the 'liberation and promises' of God that are germane to the argument here for evolution *per se* cannot offer either promise or liberation;

---

[37] "And no creature is hidden from his sight, but all are naked and exposed to the eyes of him to whom we must give account." (Hebrews 4:13) It is the imago Dei that is to be called into account not the rest of creation that, though groaning, 'looks' to its creator for its continued existence.

however the God of the Christian Bible can: The creator God whose character is such that He cares passionately for all that He has created and promises to liberate—the creation from its 'groaning'—the creation that God Himself has brought under subjugation; this subjugation though, as we shall argue, should not be thought of in a utilitarian way—as if the ephemeral appearance of the millions of creatures over the course of time were simply a means to a 'convergent' end—that [all] of creation has no value to its creator other than that of 'a means to an end'.[38] Moreover, the giving of himself in creation underlies God's character—especially his 'Triunity'. Douglas Meeks (2006) has said that the doctrine of the [social] Trinity claims that God's 'owning' is not grounded in self-possession but rather in self-giving: "It is the character of God to give God's self to us and to give us all things with God's self (Romans 8:32). God owns by giving...It is God's self-giving which, is the font of human livelihood in community." (Meeks, 18) God creates in order to show both his Glory and His Benevolence—God sharing His life with carbon based life-forms. Is that not a 'good thing?' God would have, surely 'rejoiced' in the results of the creative process that, profusely, established life in all its diversity throughout the earth, seas and skies.

It was this amazing array of life that inhabited this 'bright-blue-sphere'—eons before the arrival of mankind. Before the shadow of man's presence on earth there existed a creation that would not have been 'read' (by any extraterrestrial observer) as being 'red in tooth and claw' for there existed no carbon-based life-form that could have set itself up as judge—creation, even then, was good, in all

---

[38] Regarding the Triune God's intimate concern for creation Alister McGrath (2002) states that the Trinitarian conception of God affirms that God is to be thought of as both creator of the world and a creative presence within it, "...it *(creation)* is and remains both God's possession and the place of indwelling of the one who 'fills all in all' Ephesians 1:23." (McGrath 2002, 49)

its array. It has, though, been increasingly the case that, should a 'creator' of the cosmos be allowed, this deity would seem to be culpable—but only in the eyes of those with the wherewithal to judge. But this would have been the observation of a species without true cognizance of both the nature of creation or its benevolent creator . Prior to the advent of modern man there would not have been this 'palpable' sense of moral 'indignation' proffered against the author of creation—the creation would have been amoral in its character yet it would, nevertheless have been a 'good' creation as it would have been the creation of a benevolent deity. But this [Creation] alone: without either the emergence of the creatures that are allowed the freedom of accusation—or the appearance of the accuser [Satan] who neither loved God or acknowledged God's right to rule—could never have been a completed work—for it has been the timeless plan and the telos of God to create such a species as mankind and for God to 'put on frail flesh and die' —so that the creation could be released from its bondage to decay and Christ's victory over [moral] evil could be finally won. Ronald Osborn refers to what he describes as, "...the ancient patristic understanding of *theosis*—the view that God's purposes in creating included his desire, from the beginning for the divinization of humankind through the hominization of Christ...And the divine love has always willed that the journey of creation and pilgrimage of humanity should end in our final adoption as coheirs of God's kingdom and "partakers of the divine nature". (Osborn 2014, 159)

There are several points to be taken from the above:

God, Evolution, and Evil's Mystery
Julian Fernandes

i.   Creation through the evolutionary process is, undeniably prolific—its diversity, complexity and beauty beyond the realms of coincidence or 'coincidental convergence'.[39]

ii.   Creation declares the glory of God, and whatever declares the glory of God is a 'good thing'.

iii.   That God's concern for the creation is personal. The Triune God sustains the present creation .

iv.   That, in Christ and for Christ, God continues to prepare a created order (new heavens & new earth) so that God's ultimate good purposes shall obtain.

Prior to offering his own compound evolutionary theodicy Christopher Southgate (2008, 15) reconsiders the implications of a 'very good creation'—concluding that creation is good in its proclivity to give rise to what Southgate refers to as, "...great values of beauty, diversity, complexity, and ingenuity of evolutionary strategy...Moreover, "It is also good because it is the Lord's (Ps.24:1)"

---

[39] It is accepted that there is a chaotic element that may be defined as being without a blueprint (Dawkins 2009) or that there may be chaotic interference that might be considered the work of other hands (Mathew 13:28).

Step 2. Such a world can only arise via an evolutionary process, which also necessitates suffering and apparent waste:

In a chapter entitled 'Evolutionary explanation' Ian Hutchinson (**2011**) refers to the dangers of a hospital environment. Hutchinson comments that one reason hospitals are such dangerous places is that, "…the environmental pressures on the bacteria there *(in hospitals)* are such that they rapidly evolve resistance to the various anti-bacterial agents that hospitals use." (**96**) Within the evolutionary 'framework' there are a quite remarkable amount of life-forms, some of which might be considered unnecessary intruders, or the kinds of creation that God would 'surely not have conjured-up' because they seem to prove a contradiction in terms when one maintains a particular understanding of what a 'good' creation would look like. Bacterial life-forms are, as Hutchinson infers, endemic—not only in hospitals but in the whole of the biosphere. They are essential to the whole of the history of the biosphere. Michael Behe (**2007, 63**) refers to statistics offered by workers at the University of Georgia who estimated that about a billion billion trillion (10^{30}) bacterial cells are formed on the earth each and every year. Dennis Alexander (**2008, 277**) refers to the necessary effects of biological evolution on its products—advocating that biology is a package deal and that the values only come with the disvalues. However, Alexander goes on to say that the positive side of this is that we are living in an incredibly dynamic world in which there is what he refers to as 'a huge amount of daily coming and going—the dead of all kinds are constantly making room for the living; all of life is Interdependent' (**279-280**). Alexander holds that the God of all creation is also the great naturalist who enjoys all the richness and diversity of the natural world that he has brought into being—including its 'impressive carnivores' (**281**)[40]. Polkinghorne underlines the fact that this current universe is a creation endowed with the physical properties that have empowered it to 'make itself' over the course of its evolutionary history:

> A world of this kind by its necessary nature must be a world of transience in which death is the cost of new life. In theological terms, this world is a creation that is sustained by its Creator, and which has been endowed with a divinely purposed fruitfulness,..." (**2002, 114**)

God is not, as Polkinghorne affirms elsewhere, the tyrannical puppeteer of the universe. This world may be endowed by collaboration and fruitfulness but it is also a 'vale of tears' in which, metaphorically speaking, 'all hell breaks loose'. Such a world as this most definitely necessitates suffering, but whether or not its proclivity to produce the 'short successes' of life—the inevitability of pain and extinction may be considered wasteful may not be comprehensively addressed from mankind's current perspective. God is, as Polkinghorne suggests, "...the One who holds creation in being and interacts in hidden ways with its history." (**114**) What may be observed 'today' is not the whole story. Polkinghorne refers to the, "two halves of God's great creative/redemptive act..." (**120**)—the second half being that through which God shall bring about both vindication and justification for the [Created] state of affairs. The 'present' half (the old creation) may be seen to explore and realise its potentiality at "some metaphysical distance

---

[40] Alexander's 'picture' of the 'great naturalist' enjoying the sight of one section of his handiwork tearing apart the other is not one that speaks of benevolence, but rather of a sort of divine utilitarianism. The utilitarian view is one that could only be considered in the absence of divine benevolence, which is in contradistinction to the view held here—benevolence being a key part of the argument.

God, Evolution, and Evil's Mystery
Julian Fernandes

from its Creator" **(116)** while the second half—the new redeemed creation—is brought into freedom through its intimate relationship with the 'life of God'—in and through the work of Christ.

In philosophy much is spoken of regarding the existence of a 'Best Possible World'—that in order to offer a defence for the existence of evil in the world this world is to be defined as 'the best possible world'. In referring to the supreme wisdom of the God of Scripture, Leibniz states that, "...supreme wisdom—united to a goodness that is no less infinite cannot but have chosen the best..." (Theodicy, 197) In other words, the God of the Bible would have had to create the best possible world. Ergo, this world is the best [of] possible states of affairs. But is that the case? Moreover, need it be so? Southgate (2008) says that he fully accepts that, "...we can never be sure that this was God's only way to give rise to creatures such as stem from the 3.8-billion-year-long evolution of the Earth's biosphere." (30) However, Southgate goes on to say that, "...given what we know about creatures, especially what we know about the role of evolution, in refining their characteristics, and the sheer length of time the process has required to give rise to sophisticated sentience, it is eminently plausible and coherent to conclude that this was the only way open to God." (2008, 30)

It might be suggested that Southgate is sacrificing the omnipotence of God in order to retain God's benevolence. However, there are several things that can be said in answer to this. Firstly, in the light of our comprehension of the evolutionary process so far, we can ascertain certain fundamentals of the evolutionary process—fundamentals that Southgate mentions above: a) the role of evolution in the refining of creature's characteristics, b) the amount of time taken. Given the nature of God's omnipotence we can presume that the time and

God, Evolution, and Evil's Mystery
Julian Fernandes

procedure had nothing to do with God's ability but all to do with God's planned intentions to produce intelligent carbon-based-life on this planet. Given God's benevolence we can further assume that there was no 'better' way for God to bring about/to actualise particular outcomes.[41] Critics demand to know why it is that, in spite of God's 'alleged' attributes, this world appears to fall far short of being the 'best possible world'. Michael Murray (2008) considers two sorts of criticism: i. that the natural laws could have been better and ii. that there could have been more 'evil-preventing interventions'. Murray suggest that, "To show that such a world is possible the critic would need to describe a nomically regular world which (a) contains goodness of the sorts (either the same sorts or equivalent or better sorts) and amounts found in the actual world and which (b) contains substantially less natural evil than the actual world." (147) Murray's conclusion is that the task seems hopeless—that it would be necessary to identity a reasonably complete list of the goods that this actual world contains in order to offer a 'best possible world' potentiality. Murray suggests that it would be hard to know whether or not the acquisition of such a comprehensive list was at all possible. "Not only must the critic confront the fact that describing such an alternative world is seemingly beyond our capacities, she must also confront the claims of numerous scientists that there are many respects in which the physical parameters governing our world could not, after all, be significantly different from what they are in fact." (2008, 147) Murray's points are crucial to the question of whether or not God could have presented a better option. The argument presented here is that Murray is correct—as from our present

---

[41] The particular outcome being the 'birth' and development of the species that have the freedom to choose or not to choose—Imago Dei. It is this perspective of evolution, *id est* the freedom of the Imago Dei to respond to the love of God that is 'P' here. Moreover, it has been the ascent of man that has provided a 'highway for our God'—Immanuel with us.

understanding of the physical world—we cannot know whether or not there could have been a better option; this world being de facto the world we inhabit and of which we have reasonably comprehensive knowledge. Most importantly, it is because of the character of the God of Scripture, that we can assume that this world is the best of possible worlds. Liebniz indeed argues (197) that it is in this sense that this world is the best possible world, as we know of no other, and assume that God would not have created this world without it being an absolute necessary state of affairs; this is, as is suggested above, an assumption rather than an argument—is though a reasonable assumption. Alvin Plantinga (1974, 44), quite rightfully, points out that Leibniz' view (*his lapse*) that an omnipotent God could have created/actualised just any world God pleased is false; this is taken to mean that, according to this reasoning, God could have created a world in which there was neither natural or moral evil. This world, as is painfully obvious, contains states of affairs that are considered to be rather bad states of affairs—affairs that, it can be concluded are brought about by both 'natural' and 'moral' evil. However, this world **is** the best possible world, in that it is in this kind of environment in which the freedom of the action of carbon-based life expresses itself and in which the actions of both men and angels have both good and bad outcomes. If God were to create a world in which there existed only good outcomes, it would not be a world in which freedom could, in real terms, express itself because neither an action or an outcome would have moral veracity as both would be neutral—neither good or bad. It is in this, the best of possible worlds, that the first part of Polkinghorne's (2002) two-stage act of God's creation plan can be actualised: The first-stage being the present scenario—subject to the effects of entropy, and the second-stage following on from the eschaton—'new heavens and earth'. Polkinghorne's scenario though does not offer a defence for God's use of the evolutionary process but rather brings a focus on a future (eschatological) finality where all may be considered 'well'.

Listed in what he refers to as the core of his approach Christopher Southgate states that there is a strong likelihood that, "...an evolving creation was the only way in which God could give rise to the sort of beauty, diversity, sentience, and sophistication of creatures that the biosphere now contains." (2008, 16) Southgate qualifies this by stating that this is, indeed, an '(unprovable) assumption'. Given that the overwhelming consensus of both science and philosophy is that evolution is the most likely means through which all carbon-based-life came into existence then it is extremely likely that Southgate is correct in his assessment. However, it is not 'just' that an evolutionary 'creative' process has been the only way through which such a rich tapestry of life could have developed; it is also the case that, because of the biospheric potentiality, the evolution of creatures with the potential for higher-order-thought—the emergence of the Imago Dei would have been a most likely outcome.

From a theistic-evolutionary perspective, it can be said that it [Evolution] has been the means through which God has brought about the best possible outcomes—for His [good] purposes. Of course, that the [Darwinian] evolutionary process can be described as either directed or good is hotly disputed—especially by those who deny either the existence of God or of any such 'good outcomes' that God might [bring] about through the evolutionary process. The perspective taken in this thesis is that of 'Evolutionary Creationism'—described by Denis O. Lamoureux as "a *purpose-driven natural process* (2013, 43)". It is assumed, therefore, that God does bring about his created objectives—even through what appears to be random processes.

God, Evolution, and Evil's Mystery

Julian Fernandes

Dennis Alexander (2008) posed the question of how a good God could choose to bring about all of the biological diversity, including us—'by such a long and wasteful process—a process that involves so much death and suffering?' (277). Alexander goes on to say that the positive side of this is that we are living in an incredibly dynamic world in which there is what Alexander refers to as 'a huge amount of daily coming and going—the dead of all kinds are constantly making room for the living; all of life is Interdependent' (279-280). Alexander holds that the God of all creation is also the great naturalist who enjoys all the richness and diversity of the natural world that he has brought into being—including its 'impressive carnivores' (281). However, Alexander's picture of the 'great naturalist' enjoying the sight of one section of his handiwork tearing apart the other is not one that speaks of benevolence, rather of a sort of divine utilitarianism. But, the question is: Is the process simply a means to an end—and what end might that be?

The theological problem with which this thesis wrestles is that of suffering within evolution. Southgate (**2008, 7**) notes that this problem has several aspects. One is that if God created this system, which is full of suffering, then the goodness of God seems to be in question. But another is the question just raised in respect of Alexander's work: Did God *use* suffering within evolution as a means to the divine ends? Alister McGrath (**2011**) brings the issue into focus by noting that Darwin's model of evolution envisages the emergence of the animal kingdom as taking place over a vastly extended period of time, involving suffering and apparent wastage that go far beyond the concerns of traditional theodicy. (**202**). McGrath notes that Darwinism intensifies existing concerns with the problem of suffering. With evolution comes suffering and death—they are a part of the same

God, Evolution, and Evil's Mystery
Julian Fernandes

package. If God is able to create all the necessary material and has the wherewithal to envisage and bring into being the best possible world—and yet has, seemingly, failed to accomplish his objectives without huge concomitant suffering then there are bona fide reasons for seeking answers as to why this seems not to be the case. As has been stated previously, the prevailing view is that a (system of biological evolutionary development) is the only way through which all the 'values' of all the creatures that have ever existed could obtain. Ergo: predation, pain, parasitism, plague and (obviously) death are all instrumental in the processes that produce the values to which Southgate refers. Southgate argues that the sort of universe we witness, "...in which complexity emerges in a process governed by thermodynamic necessity and Darwinian natural selection, and therefore by pain, predation, and self-assertion, is the only sort of universe that could give rise to the range, beauty, complexity, and diversity of creatures the Earth has produced." **(2008, 29)** As has been said previously, Southgate fully accepts that it is not possible to know whether or not the evolution of the Earth's biosphere was God's only way. Nevertheless it is as, Southgate suggests, plausible to suppose that the evolutionary process was God's only way.[42] However, that God had the 'one option' (that of biological evolution) does not preclude the likelihood of God's omnipotence or that God might be an 'under achiever' but rather that God's desire was to bring about a state of affairs that allowed for the evolution of carbon based life forms—a creation with independent characteristics allowing for the 'arrival' of free-will—especially (in the case of mankind) the interaction of 'mind' and body. Daniel Dennett says the following regarding the notion of the 'evolution of free-will':

---

[42] It is the case that absolute knowledge of distant past events has to be seen through a less than absolute lens and that there is much we presume to have comprehensive knowledge of today that might be proven inaccurate in the future.

God, Evolution, and Evil's Mystery

Julian Fernandes

> Since I am conscious and you are conscious, we must have conscious selves...How can this be? To see how such an extraordinary composition job could be accomplished we need to look at the history of the design processes that did all the work—the evolution of human consciousness. We also need to see how these souls made of cellular robots actually do endow us with the important powers and resultant obligations that traditional material souls were supposed to endow us with (by unspecified magic). **(Dennett 2003, 3)**

'Magic' apart: it is the question of the notion of 'evolving' freedom that, naturally, divides opinion in evolutionary interpretation. However from a theistic perspective there need be no such tension—as John Turl points out, "Whether or not we can postulate a reasonable method of interaction, for Christians the basic datum is that pure spirit can interact with matter..." (2010, 75) Turl offers the following examples: " God, who is spirit, created the universe, which is matter (Jn. 4:24;1:3). Angels have communicated with humans (Heb.1:14; Luke 1:13,28). The Holy Spirit affects human minds (Jn. 14:26; 16:8)" (Turl, 75)[43] From a theistic perspective, Turl's conclusion is entirely reasonable—and indeed plausible. This may seem somewhat of a paradoxical state of affairs as we appear to be referring to both a process of evolution that is unguided and a Deity that is able, in ways indiscernible to any sophisticated microscope, to somehow, within the

---

[43] In his conclusion Turl points out the following:

- o   It seems difficult if not impossible to construct a non-reductive monism; reductive monism seems unacceptable philosophically and theologically.
- o   Scripture does not favour monism in preference to a dualistic account of man.

It is not necessary to assume that physics is hostile to the existence of an ontological soul. (Turl 2010, 79)

evolutionary process, bring about changes in line with His teleological objectives[44]. The point here is that there are outcomes that may be predicted and outcomes that may not. The argument in this thesis is that such a world as this can only arise via an evolutionary process, which also necessitates suffering and apparent waste. However, it is also the case that Scripture suggests a better outcome—an outcome that God has purposed from before the creation of the world—the Telos of God.

---

[44] Should God so work within the cosmos it has to be admitted that there is little evidence of God 'actively' pursuing paths that ease the suffering of the 'products' of such a state of affairs. However, should the evolutionary process have been left completely to its 'own devices', there would be no guarantee of a good outcome—especially regarding the emergence of the imago Dei, the incarnation, the victory of the Son of God over the principalities and powers...

Step 3. Only such a world is capable of being transformed into the 'new creation', in which there need be no more suffering:

Having discussed various insights into the redemptive possibilities offered by some scientists/theologians engaging in what may be described as 'eschatological conjecture', Christopher Southgate (2008, 85-90) underlines his view that, since this world is the world the God of 'all creativity and all compassion' chose for the creation of carbon-based-life-forms, we must presume that there was no other option—that, "...though heaven can eternally preserve those selves, subsisting in suffering-free relationship, it could not give rise to them in the first place." (90) Southgate's point is clear. If God could have, initially, created heaven, why did God not so do? [45] Southgate offers a clear explanation as mentioned previously—that though heaven can eternally preserve the 'selves' (in 'a new, heaven and new earth', environment) it cannot give rise to the carbon-based-life-forms that evolution has produced. Ergo, the 4 billion years or so of evolutionary development has been a necessary state of affairs.

The argument in this thesis is that for God's [good] outcomes to realise, there had to be the emergence of mankind (Imago Dei) as the 'vessel made of clay'—fit for the Spirit of God (Swinburne 1997). For the possibility of the incarnation of

---

[45] However, as Southgate would agree—and as the likes of Michael Lloyd (Are Animals Fallen? 1998) have made clear; it is not sufficient to offer a solely eschatological defence—as such defences, in their desire for scientific/philosophical acceptance, tend to be 'anti-Christian'. In other words (*my words not Lloyd's*)—the defence/theodicy that does not have Scripture as its prime source (its raison d'être).

God, Evolution, and Evil's Mystery
Julian Fernandes

the second person of the Trinity (ultimately for the Victory of God' over Evil to obtain), it necessitated the protracted process of biological evolution. For the sake of our argument here, the necessary constituents for God's planned intentions can be listed under the following brief headings:

i. The existence of the Second Law of Thermodynamics—allowing for the effects of entropy—for its necessary consequences: life, death and evolutionary selection .

ii. The evolution of Free-Will as expressed in the lives and experience of the imago Dei—the 'Telos' of [God] through evolution.

iii. The arrival of the species that Scripture describes as being made in the image of God (imago Dei).

iv. The physical appearance (incarnation), life, suffering, death and resurrection of the second person of the Trinity: Jesus Christ.

Regarding the 4 billion-year- biological-evolutionary-state-of-affairs, Adrian Hough (2010) offers some interesting and useful insights—perceptions that are germane to the argument in this thesis. Hough states that in more scientific terms we are able to say that the increase in entropy or disorder (which is a fundamental characteristic of the universe) is the cause of suffering and of death. (106) This is, most would agree, a de facto, state of affairs. Hough adds to this by asking whether the cross can also be seen as God accepting the consequences of the Second Law? Though God, we believe, would not shrink from taking whatever responsibility **is** God's, we do not accept the argument that offers the cross of Christ as some kind of 'self-punishment' for God's own failure to produce a better outcome—in particular for the billions of years of suffering 'meted out' by Natural Selection— though we do take seriously the notion that

God, Evolution, and Evil's Mystery
Julian Fernandes

this 'silent' universe somehow echoes the cry of the 'Crucified [Son] of God'. It is in this sense that the universe is cruciform, for how could the sacrifice of God the Son not reverberate throughout the universe? God, we maintain, *is not guilty* of producing a world that could have been otherwise created; this world is the only possible world; it is also the world that God intended to create, and it is in this world, and no other, that the Problem of Evil has been dealt its death blow. This world is the best possible world—in which the consequences that Hough refers to can also obtain. Yet it is also the world in which Christ can take on himself the sins of the world—of the flesh and of the devil. It is in this world that God allows the results of free-will to have, seemingly, free-reign; yet it is a world out of which can arise a different state of affairs—a world wherein the Second Law has a different functionality. Hough says that what is clear from the present consideration is that, "... the Second Law of Thermodynamics leads us to a grander vision of God if our vision of God begins with the assumption that Jesus Christ rose from the dead and that God wills the renewal of His creation." (2010, 133) [46]

Key to the argument in this thesis is that this world order (since its genesis) can be described in terms of its being the only possible world that could precede the advents of the incarnation and (at the eschaton) a 'new heaven and a new earth'. It is this world, with both its values and disvalues, that allows for a world of absolute values to obtain. It is this world that is subject to the effects of particular laws that, humans at least, have no means of controlling or of changing. This is not to say that mankind can effect no change whatsoever but

---

[46] Against the notion of a lesser deity—a 'ground of being' version of 'God' Hough suggests that, "If we consider the way in which the universe works, then it is clear that God has in some sense to be beyond the universe." (Hough 2010, 133)

that it would not be possible for mankind, *per se*, to create a heaven on earth or to change the prevailing cosmological state of affairs. It is the Triune God that promises a better state of affairs—an eschatological fulfilment of God's ultimate purposes for his creation—a creation that bears the scars of the 'Crucified God' (Moltmann 1993)[47]. Sam Storms (2013) writes that, "...the unfolding fulfilment of God's promises may be seen in terms of what Geerhardus Vos called a 'binary configuration'. That is to say, human history reflects a tension between what was accomplished at the first advent of Christ and what awaits consummation at the second." (28) Southgate (2008) refers to the insights of R.J.Russell who sees the resurrection of Jesus Christ as, "...the beginning of a final act that will transform the character of creation..." (80) Moreover Southgate and Russell along with Wolfhart Pannenberg (2008, 16, 163) advocate that, " The long sweep of evolution may not only suggest an unfinished and continuing divine creation but even more radically a creation whose theological status as 'good' may be fully realised only in the eschatological future." (80) Whilst having sympathy with the opinions of Southgate and Russell, that creation's good status may be 'identified' as being good only at the eschaton, we do not think it necessary to deny the creation its 'good' status presently; for the creation has been good from its genesis and it shall remain good throughout eternity.

It is the quest for a Theory of Everything (Wilkinson 2001)—the 'Big Picture' that fuels the desire for knowledge; and it is the 'Big Picture' that is the driving force of scientific enquiry. However, as has been said elsewhere, it is the theology that drives the quest for a defence for the goodness of God.

---

[47] "The knowledge of the cross brings a conflict of interest between God who has become man and man who wishes to become God." (Moltmann 1993)

Step 4. But also, there is evidence that angels exist:

Firstly, it should be noted that there is no need to assume that the 'time' and location of the creation of the devil and the other angels should be accounted for in the Genesis story of creation. Moreover it is important to maintain the notion of these extra-terrestrial beings as having the will to choose 'wrong' from 'right': to bring about a state of affairs that might not be the preferred will of God but that of the outworking of minds opposed to the good. There can be no reason why angels could not be endowed with the kind of abilities that, even scientists, have no present/ personal acquaintance with. Indeed, even though God is incorporeal—God, nevertheless, cannot be restricted to any particular 'reality' designated by either science or philosophy—as if God, who is spirit, could not possess, *within God's life*, such things as personality, will, intellect and 'personal existence'. Angels (both holy and unholy), though usually without form (incorporeal), may, as Scripture makes clear, inhabit the 'physicality' of carbon-based life forms. Moreover, as with God, who is Spirit, angels have personal qualities that are far superior to that of mankind's. These creatures were, according to Scripture, privileged beings with powers that far surpass those of human agents.[48] Hebrews 2:7-9 (also Psalm 8:5) refers to the 'position' of the incarnate 'son of man' who was, '...for a little while lower than the angels.' [49] N.T.Wright (1992) refers to the Shema ("Hear, O Israel: YHWH is one.")—that it is the most famous Jewish prayer, "...burned into the consciousness of Judaism in

---

[48] These references pertain to the 'position & power' of angels: Psalm 34:7; Psalm 82:1 ; 1 Chronicles 21:15; Isaiah 37:36, 63:9; Ezekiel chapters 1 & 10. Ezekiel 28. The book of Revelation is replete with examples of such creatures as angels. Genesis 6 also makes mention of their being creatures other than humans 'on earth'; this it can be assumed was a reference to pre-history.

[49] As Christ was made in the form of a man and had subjected himself to this position (Philippians 2:7,8); he, temporarily, had made himself 'lower than the angels'.

the first century and that it was the battle cry of the nation that believed its god to be the only god, supreme in heaven and on earth…"However, as we shall argue in this section, God's so being in no way precludes the existence of created agents—agents that may be referred to as: 'god's, 'angels' or 'spiritual beings'—the existence of such created beings is, unlike some forms of Dualism, not a challenge or denial of the sovereignty of the God of Scripture.

Ulrich Mauser (1991) argued that the supremacy of Israel's God over all other gods—though everywhere asserted—is not a denial the existence of such 'gods'. Boyd argues that, whilst strongly advocating the sovereignty of Yahweh, the Old Testament does include the understanding that, "…Yahweh [must] contend with a sometimes disobedient and incompetent council of spiritual beings (usually called 'gods'), and must in fact contend with one particularly malicious god entitled 'the adversary'." (Boyd 1997, 115) Boyd points out that any reality regarding the struggle with other 'gods' is never taken to compromise the supremacy and sovereignty of Yahweh but rather it is taken to express the way in which Yahweh *is* supreme and sovereign. Boyd makes clear however that the Israelites did not deny the existence of angelic or spiritual beings but rather that these beings (angelic or spiritual) were referred to as 'gods'—moreover Boyd also makes clear that these creatures possessed a great deal of autonomous power.

Christopher Southgate says that, "…whatever processes science is able to understand as contributing to the evolution of complexity, life, richness of ability and diversity in life, and the growth of self-consciousness and freedom of choice, must be presumed to be the gift of God in creation." **(2008, 33)** It is the case that such creativity must emanate in the mind of God, and so it is not at all implausible that this should be the case with extra-terrestrial beings. The existence of angelic beings need not be considered a threat to either science or, indeed, to God's sovereignty. Angels are as much a part of God's creative will as anything else God may have created. Richard Swinburne's **(1996)** view is that "God has no obligation to create". **(97)** God creates in freedom—to offer the freedom of choice that the creation of conscious/sentient beings allows for — even when this freedom entails an element of risk in terms of the outcomes of any choice. The Sovereignty of the God of Scripture does not entail submission of all of creation to a defined pathway. God is free to choose to create or not to create extraterrestrial and terrestrial beings and any and every biological, or unknown, expression of his creativity. Creation, through the evolutionary process or any other means, is God's prerogative alone—though Scripture suggests that God may delegate that responsibility to lesser beings as James J.Grenshaw points out **(2005, 50)**.

Job 1:6 informs us that 'the sons of God' presented themselves before God and that Satan 'came among them'[50] .We are not told exactly where the place of meeting (Council of God) was located. It is however reasonable to assume that it was to be found somewhere outside of the physical universe—at least the 'known cosmos'[51] .Grenshaw states that, "Allusions to this heavenly court can be found in texts of various genres, beginning in Genesis and continuing through much of the Bible." **(2005, 50)** Moreover, Grenshaw argues that the peoples of the ancient

---

[50] Robert Sutherland says that, "As a member of the heavenly host and not yet an outside challenger, he seems to have unlimited access to God and the divine council." (Sutherland 2004, 33)

[51] There are numerous scriptures that evidence a 'heavenly council e.g. '...let us go down...' (Genesis 11:7); Isaiah's vision of God (Isaiah 6); 'Ascribe to the Lord O heavenly beings,...' (Psalm 29:1); 'From heaven your stars fought, from their courses they fought against Sisera.' (Judges 5:20); '...Bring down your warriors, O Lord...' (Joel 3:11)

God, Evolution, and Evil's Mystery
Julian Fernandes

Near East conceived of the gods—and of these 'gods' as forming a heavenly assembly, "...a kind of divine council..." (**2005**) Psalm 82:1 says that, "'God' has taken his place in the divine council; in the midst of the gods he holds judgement." Grenshaw refers to both these texts (Job 1:6 and psalm 82:1)—particularly regarding the use of the word '*elohim*'—as , "...a telling sign that the polytheistic world of the Bible was understood to be more than simply a literary construct." (**50**)The point here is that the notion of other 'gods' relates to extra-terrestrial-created-agents—agents also described in Scripture as angelic.

Regarding the existence of the angelic hosts John Lennox (2011) refers to the 'unannounced arrival' of the serpent in Genesis 3—a creature that was clearly opposed to God; a creature that could be described as an 'alien'—not a biological entity but something extra-terrestrial in origin. Unlike biological entities, angels do not appear to have a 'shelf-life'—they seem to be much more durable than the normal created entities, such as humankind, and may, as they are incorporeal (unless 'inhabiting some other life-form),not subject to the effects of entropy as experienced by carbon based creatures. They don't 'rust or decay'—they just exist in another realm in the cosmos or—even in a 'dimension' as yet undetectable by man or machine. Somehow these 'creatures' are given access to this space/time continuum and seem able to do both good and evil—to produce 'good outcomes' and 'harmful outcomes'. The point here is that such creatures are unlike, anything else in all creation, capable of powerful influence within the physical universe—especially here on earth. Ergo, they are formidable adversaries—opposing any good outcomes and encouraging or devising outcomes to the contrary.

God, Evolution, and Evil's Mystery
Julian Fernandes

Richard Middleton (**2005**) observes that, although the plurals: 'Let us make man in our image, in our likeness,' (Genesis 1:26-28) have been interpreted as 'a remnant of a polytheistic mythology [referring to the gods of the Canaanite or Mesopotamian pantheon], and adumbration of the Trinity—or at least of a plurality within the Godhead or several other alternatives, a careful intertextual reading of the plurals in Genesis 1:26 suggests that God here addresses the heavenly court or divine council of angels, a reading first suggested in rabbinic commentary on Genesis 1, going back to the 'Targum Pseudo-Jonathan' (**55**)[52]. Middleton also states that in many biblical texts[53], God's throne room is associated with a heavenly court of angelic beings, who are royal messengers of the cosmic king and who function as God's attendants or counselors. (**56**) Moreover, Middleton points out that 'the main action' no longer occurs in the heavens:

> Rather, the dramatic movement of the text is from the heavens (days 1 and 4) to the waters (days 2 and 5) to the earth (days 3 and 6), which is the focus for four of God's eight creative acts. This may explain why on day 6, which foregrounds the *earth*, there is no explicit vision (or mention) of *heavenly* beings. Yet their presence is alluded to by the shift from third-person jussives in God's first seven creative acts to the other cryptic cohortative ('let us make') in the eighth act. (Middleton, 56) [54]

---

[52] 'Targum Pseudo-Jonathan rests on a tradition going back to pre-Christian times, though its final form is probably sixth century C,E.' (Middleton 2005, p.55fn)

[53] Job 1:6;2:1;5:1;15:8;38:7;Psalm 29:1;82:1;89:5-7;97:7;Exodus 15:11;2 Samuel 5:22-25:1 Kings 22:19; Isaiah 6: 2-8;Jeremiah 23:18, 21-22;Ezekiel 1:312-13;10;Daniel 4:17 etc.

[54] Isaiah 6:8 is another example of a similar first-person plural—'Whom shall I send, and who will go for us?' (ESV)

Middleton's point is that angelic beings[55] are not foreign to the author of Genesis 1 'as is indicated by the occurrence of similar first-person plurals in 3:22 and 11:7 (both of which are usually regarded unproblematically as referring to the heavenly court).' (57) In other words, it can be assumed <u>that</u> there was some kind of plural communication—if not co-operation—in the act of creation's genesis at least. Besides the Spirit of God—some of the 'hosts of heaven' were present on the earth at the very dawn of the birth of life on earth. The witness of certain New Testament passages is that he whom the Church came to confess as the second person of the Trinity was present (Colossians 1:15-20 & Hebrews 1:1-3;10-13).

Simon Gathercole (2006, 114) refers to what he terms an 'I have come + purpose formula'—as in the pronouncements of Angels. The use of this formula is, Gathercole states, 'not to be understood idiomatically'—as an intrusion into the earthly realm but as a 'coming with prior intent...Gathercole offers a helpful summary:

> Angels announce their advents with the 'I have come' + purpose formula. They can do this: a) because they are summarizing *not* their whole *existence* (they visit on numerous occasions) but the purpose of a particular visit; b) because they have a pre-existence in heaven. Similarly, Jesus announces his advent with the 'I have come' + purpose formula because he is summarizing the purpose of his whole *earthly life* and ministry. As with the angels, Jesus is not summarizing his whole *existence* (he will come again, with different purposes). However, he does summarize his life's work with the 'I have come' + purpose formula...
> (Gathercole 2006, 117)

---

[55] Contrary to some objections—objections that Middleton considers implausible. e.g. Westermann, Genesis,1.pp.144-45

God, Evolution, and Evil's Mystery
Julian Fernandes

Peter S. Williams offers, what he describes as, a set of proposed 'explananda':

1. The majority of humanity believes in angels.

2. The majority of philosophers believe in angels.

3. There are various paranormal phenomena that would be coherently and economically explained if demons exist.

4. There are multiple historical and contemporary reports by evidently honest and intelligent eyewitnesses (including psychologists, psychiatrists and clergy) to the reality of Angels and demonic possession (including Satanic possession).

5. The Bible teaches that Angels and demons (including Gabriel, Michael and Satan) exist (and we have good reason to trust what the Bible teaches).

6. Christian tradition teaches that Angels and demons (including Satan) exist.

7. Jesus teaches that Angels and demons (including Satan) exists (and we have good reason to trust what Jesus teaches.

8. The hypothesis that demons exist provides a partial explanation of *how it is* that God and evil are compatible realities.

9. Given the existence of God, there is a continuous pattern of hierarchy in creation that seems to come to a unique, aesthetically abrupt and unexpected end, unless angels exist. (P. Williams 2002, 142-143)

It is therefore reasonable to suppose that it is the case that Angels exist and that they have a continual influence over both good and bad outcomes. It is also the case that God allows such creatures the freedom to choose either good or bad—to love and serve God or to deny God any allegiance whatsoever.

God, Evolution, and Evil's Mystery
Julian Fernandes

Given the above detail, we can more than assume that the intelligence, knowledge etc. of angels does not 'emanate' from any primordial source, Moreover, it can be supposed that these creatures are personal beings rather than vague concepts—oppressive systems, power oriented ideals [mores] etc. We can further assume that they are not restricted to act in the way 'material' objects may be considered/constrained so to act.

God, Evolution, and Evil's Mystery
Julian Fernandes

Step 5. That Angels may have existed before the creation of this universe:

The likelihood that Angels pre-existed the advent of the evolution of the 13.7 billion year-old physical creation is both plausible and coherent. Regarding the question of whether or not angels began when matter began Peter Kreeft (1995) suggests that 'angel time' is not the time of the material universe and that angels are no more in physical time than they are in 'physical space'—as matter is. Kreeft's argument (and ours) is that angels have to enter into this world from without: "We cannot use the standards of time from this universe—either the revolutions of the 'heavenly' bodies or the constant speed of light to measure how old angels are. Material time is a function of matter, is relative to matter. It does not exist before matter exists. It is between eternity and time."

(Kreeft, 92-93) As angels are incorporeal they are not material. Ergo, they were not created through a process of biological evolution and are not, apart from when possessing materiality (*possessing the physical*) in any way subject to physical laws. There are however contrary opinions regarding creatures such as angels. Christopher Southgate (2008, 38) refers to the work of Andrew Elphinstone who regarded the demonic as something evolving out of the 'necessities of creative process'—not as 'a pre-existent being or beings'. The argument here though is that there is no need whatsoever to suppose that angels were the products of 'the impersonal, plus time plus chance'. Angels were meant to be, and existed prior to the beginnings we read of in the Genesis creation account. There can be no reason why an omnipotent God could not have, in another 'reality', other than space/time, created beings that pre-existed the creation of this [our] universe. Indeed, if there were/are in existence other created but non-carbon-based-life-forms, it is reasonable to suppose that they would have been created/existed prior to the creation of the biosphere. As angels are incorporeal creatures and as they were 'there' (Job 38:7[56]) at the dawn of creation—they would not have been a part of the evolutionary process—for if they had they surely could not have 'emerged' until some point in the future rather than the distant, pre-historical, past. God, when putting Job in his place, asks Job where he was when the morning stars sang together and all the sons of God shouted for Joy?' (Job 38:4-7). Angels pre-exist the creation of the cosmos—as has been said—there no actual record of their creation in Scripture.[57]

---

[56] "...when the morning stars sang together and all the sons of God shouted for joy?"

[57] An argument might be that these creatures were created when 'the heavens were created' (Genesis 1:1)—that the angels were created during the creation of the heavens (*shamayim*). However, this view is highly speculative at the least as the actual 'time' of their creation is not given in the Genesis text.

Step 6. That it is a good thing that God gave angels freedom:

(Irenaeus) held that, In the beginning God formed Adam, not as if He stood in need of man, but that God might have someone on which to confer his benefits. God's conferring of his benefits though does not exclude creatures other than mankind; this could apply to other sentient beings—and it could also apply to non-carbon-based-life-forms such as angels. The question here is whether God's use of angels is purely utilitarian—*are* they merely automatons—messengers, servants, aids? The argument here is that angels were not created for purely utilitarian reasons; moreover angels are not automatons. Angels are created, among other things, to worship God—something, in which, Scripture implies (e.g. Isaiah 6 Revelation 4), is found absolute fulfilment. Angels are able to benefit from the most worthwhile/worthy of all activities because they are conscious creatures with mental states such as: sensation, thought, belief, desire and act of will (active volition power). (P. Williams 2002, 80 - 86)

Swinburne (1998) says that if freedom and responsibility are good things, it is good that there be angels who have it as well as humans. The point is that: If any or all actions performed by the created order (whether angels or humans) were entirely the 'programmed' results of a divine puppet master—this could not possibly be a good state of affairs—not even for God. Swinburne argues that,"...if it is good that God should give us the ultimate choice over the period of our lives on Earth of being able to fix our characters beyond further change, it would seem to be similarly good that God should give to angels also the ultimate choice of being able to fix their characters. (108)

God, Evolution, and Evil's Mystery

Julian Fernandes

Regarding the likelihood of free-will and the existence of an omnipotent, omniscient, benevolent God, Eleonore Stump (2012) refers to the argument that states that any notion of a human tendency to moral wrongdoing is incomparable with the existence of the God who is omnipotent, omniscient and benevolent. Stump's argument can equally be applied to free-will in angels. The argument is as follows:

1. Humans *also angels (our inclusion)* have a propensity to moral wrongdoing.
2. A propensity to moral wrongdoing is itself an evil.
3. If there is a perfectly good, omnipotent, omniscient God, he would prevent or eliminate any evil in the world unless he had a morally sufficient reason to allow it.
4. There is no morally sufficient reason for God to allow the human (*angelic*) propensity to moral wrongdoing.
5. Therefore, there is no perfectly good, omnipotent, omniscient God. (153)

Stump's conclusion on the matter is that, "...to suggest that *[allowing]* any propensity to moral wrongdoing is itself evil *is mistaken.*" (153) Stump is surely correct. Why should a perfectly good God disallow the sentient creature (man or angel) such potentiality—whether for good or evil? A world in which there were no meaningful actions—actions with consequences—could not, in our opinion, be considered the best possible 'outcome' for God's creativity. For such a world, though full of diversity, complexity and beauty, would be a rather 'grey' state of affairs—lacking both meaning and opportunity. A world in which God prevented any 'bad' outcomes by, either intervening before any such morally reprehensible action could issue forth, or by rescuing the victims from their harmful effects, would be a world in which free-will was impossible or a world in which God acted as a kind of 'superman'. Should the above state of affairs obtain, <u>Free-Will</u> would, de facto, be an illusion—for actions would have no [authentic] consequences—either good or bad.

The argument in this thesis is that God's allowing his created agents (Angels and Men) free will as opposed to putting constraints on their potentiality is a good thing—as opposed to a bad thing. There is, from the perspective of this argument, no neutral position: it is good or it is bad. It is the case, however, that the freedom to choose allows for bad outcomes. Regarding the free-will choice of angels, P.S. Williams (2002), quoting an Aristotelian assay, offers the following view:

> Just as there are good houses and bad houses, so there are good and bad angels. However, while the house has no say in its value, the character of an angel is the character it has freely chosen. That an angel has the freedom to make this choice is a good thing, because it is a pre-condition of the value of freely choosing to love God and fulfil its *telos*. However, the exercise of angelic free will to reject God is a bad thing, a frustration of the angelic *telos* that results in the corruption of the intended angelic nature that is called 'demonic';... (P. Williams 2002, 110-111)

6.1 Free Will, Angels and Sovereignty

God's allowing angels free will raises the question of Sovereignty. How can God retain sovereignty while allowing the potential for what could be described as, unrestrained freedom? Indeed, what [exactly] is meant by the expression, 'The Sovereignty of God?' A.W. Pink's answer is unequivocal.

God, Evolution, and Evil's Mystery

Julian Fernandes

Pink states that, "We mean the supremacy of God, the kingship of God, the Godhead of God. To say that God is sovereign is to say that God is God. To say that God is sovereign is to declare that He is the Most High...To say that God is sovereign is to declare that He is the Almighty, the Possessor of all power in heaven and earth, so that none can defeat His counsels, thwart His purposes, or resist His will." (Pink 1980, 20) Pink's view allows for the kind of sovereignty that is not 'all controlling' but a sovereignty that depicts all the aforementioned characteristics of the Triune God. However, the term 'resist His will' may not give the best of impressions—as if God's desire is to 'control' rather than allow genuine expressions of freedom. Christian theism, Alvin Plantinga (2011, 172) argues, involves the idea that God governs the world; that what happens does not come about by chance, but by virtue of God's 'providential governance'. In other words, God is sovereign over his creation. This does not, in our opinion, mean that God controls every single event within every single minute of every single hour; or that God pre-ordains the thoughts and actions of men and of angels. There are numerous outcomes in the world that come about by either the free-will actions of agents or by the 'happenstances' of natural events. It is as David Johnstone makes clear when he refers to the weather as an example of exactly this.

> Consider the weather. The Bible is quite clear that God is in control of the weather (Psalm 42:7; Psalm 135:6-7; Psalm 148:8; Jeremiah 10:13). But we also know that the weather is a natural process. We know about the hydrological cycle and meteorologists are able to predict the weather with some success (the atmosphere being a chaotic system which makes it very hard to predict, but that is beside the point). (Johnstone 2009)

God, Evolution, and Evil's Mystery
Julian Fernandes

The point here is that the weather is a natural process, but this does not mean that God is not in control of it or not able to control it—or, in other words 'able to act sovereignly over it'. In his article entitled 'The Necessity of Chance' Paul Ewart (2009) provides good reason why perceived random events do not eradicate the notion of sovereignty, *id est* God's ability to bring about his purposes: "The necessity of chance is seen to be not just an accidental outcome of the laws of nature but an intentional aspect of God's creating process that preserves both our freedom and his freedom to act." (Ewart, 129) Of course, theological libraries are replete with books arguing for or against the sovereignty of God. The question is, however: What exactly can we infer from such a belief when contemplating the state of the world we inhabit and, indeed, the very existence of natural evil within the evolutionary paradigm?

It could be said that, if God is to be sovereign over all his creation, it must mean that God has access to it all, whether it is the known universe or otherwise. God could not, logically, be sovereign over any entity that is outside of his 'reach'. However, God's sovereignty does not necessitate a strong measure of control on God's part; rather, sovereignty means that God is sufficiently confident in his purposes immanent or eschatological for his universe—that the best of possible outcomes will obtain. Indeed this applies to the outcome of the choices of created agents. Greg Boyd refers to a common objection regarding, what he denotes as 'God's risk taking'. Boyd says that if God must risk the fate of individuals, it seems that he must also risk his overall goal of acquiring a bride. In other words, it is likely that God's entire plans for world history could ultimately fail. (2001, 146) According to this view, God could lose the fight. Boyd's is a possible conclusion from reflection on God's desire to be in loving relationship with freely-choosing creatures. However, it is difficult to imagine that the sovereign God of the universe would allow any adversary the final 'victory'. It can be argued that free-will choices have unpredictable outcomes but it is not implausible to suggest that God cannot bring about the best of possible outcomes for his creation—whether or not God has foreknowledge of those outcomes[58]. It was C.S.Lewis (2001) who stated that what is 'praiseworthy' about God's sovereignty is not that he exercises a power he obviously has but that out of his character he does not exercise all the power he could. Ergo: God is not a controlling 'god' but a God who allows 'freedom to choose' yet will, somehow, enable his plans and purposes to obtain. It may be a present mystery but it is, nevertheless, a possibility that God can so act.

Christopher Tiegreen (2006, 42) says that, somehow, God's sovereignty is woven into free will and that free will is woven into God's sovereignty. Tiegreen is referring to humanity but it can also be applied to the action of angelic 'free agents' who have the capability to bring the utmost good or to unleash the most horrendous evil. It is the case that the free-will choices of agents (angels and men) can bring about satisfactory states of affairs, *i.e.* states of affairs that may be considered good states of affairs and not bad states of affairs, but it also the case that such choices may bring about bad states of affairs. Nevertheless God's allowing for creatures with free will is, indeed, a good thing. Indeed it is as Richard Swinburne points out that, " We value the spontaneous pursuit of the

---

[58] Regarding the free will choices of humans, Henri Blocher raises a concern when he says: "Either God does not interfere and no longer has control over anything much; or else God contrives to limit the consequences of human choice, and so is not really playing the game and is reducing the drama of freedom to a superficial effect of no importance." (1994, 59). Blocher has a point—but not a significant one. The problem is in the notion that 'control' and 'sovereignty' are somehow synonymous. Can we not conceive of a God who is so great that he dares to create agents who can, to some extent, make autonomous decisions?

good, the pursuit of the good which the agent *(angels in this case)* fully desires to follow. We value the willingly generous action, the naturally honest, spontaneously loving action. But we value even more that the pursuit of the good should result from a free choice of the agent between equally good actions, that is, one resulting from the exercise of (libertarian) free will. It is good for any agent to have such free choice; for that makes him an ultimate source of the way things happen in the Universe." (Swinburne 1998, 84). Swinburne further argues that it is likely that the actions of angels may well intervene 'in an already created order' (108). [59] The possibility of such intervention is indeed plausible — though not a part of this argument. The argument in this thesis being that Angels possess free will and that this is a good state of affairs as opposed to a bad state of affairs.

---

[59] We take Swinburne to mean <u>the present order</u> rather than any pre-existing order of creation that may or may not have been carbon based.

God, Evolution, and Evil's Mystery
Julian Fernandes

Part 7. That angels rebelled and continued to oppose God's will for humans and the rest of creation:

> The devil's sin consisted of his having desired his happiness in a disordered way. But he could have understood the nature of his happiness at the first moment of his creation. Therefore, he could also have willed his happiness in a disordered way at the first moment of his creation. Any efficient cause not acting out of natural necessity can avoid what it causes. (Aquinas)

Anselm of Canterbury, (T. Williams 2013) posed the following question, which we quote in full:

> If free choice is the power to hold on to what is fitting and expedient, and it is not the power to sin, does it make any sense to say that the first human beings and the rebel angels sinned through free choice?" Anselm's reply to this question is both subtle and plausible. In order to be able to preserve rectitude of will for its own sake, an agent must be able to perform an action that has its ultimate origin in the agent him—or herself rather than in some external source...Any being that has freedom of choice, therefore, will thereby have the power for self-initiated action...Nonetheless, free choice does not entail the power to sin...In On the Fall of the Devil (De casu diaboli) Anselm extends his account of freedom and sin by discussing the first sin of the angels. In order for the angels to have the power to preserve rectitude of will for its own sake, they had to have both a will for justice and a will for happiness. If God had given them only a will for happiness, they would have been necessitated to will whatever they thought would make them happy. Their willing of

happiness would have had its ultimate origin in God and not in the angels themselves. So they would not have had the power for self-initiated action, which means that they would not have had free choice. The same thing would have been true, mutatis mutandis, if God had given them only the will for justice. (T. Williams, 4.2)

As Williams suggests, Anslem's reply is both subtle and plausible. Free-Will does not necessitate 'rebellion against authority [God] or a predilection to err'—as if either were written in the DNA of the agent, but it does allow for the potentiality of such a state of affairs. According to Scripture there is an existent state of affairs.[60]

7.1 Fallen Angels

How you are fallen from heaven, O Day Star, son of Dawn!

How you are cut down to the ground, you who laid the nations low!

---

[60] Of course this raises the question of 'Holy Angels' and their proclivity 'not to sin'. On this matter Anselm offers the following: "Since God gave them both wills, however, they had the power for self-initiated action. Whether they chose to subject their wills for happiness to the demands of justice or to ignore the demands of justice in the interest of happiness, that choice had its ultimate origin in the angels; it was not received from God. The rebel angels chose to abandon justice in an attempt to gain happiness for themselves, whereas the good angels chose to persevere in justice even if it meant less happiness. God punished the rebel angels by taking away their happiness; he rewarded the good angels by granting them all the happiness they could possibly want. For this reason, the good angels are no longer able to sin. Since there is no further happiness left for them to will, their will for happiness can no longer entice them to overstep the bounds of justice. Thus Anselm finally explains what it is that perfects free choice so that it becomes unable to sin." *(T. Williams 2013, 4.2)*

God, Evolution, and Evil's Mystery

Julian Fernandes

> You said in your heart, "I will ascend to heaven;
>
> above the stars of God; I will set my throne on high;
>
> I will sit on the mount of assembly in the far reaches of the north;
>
> I will ascend above the heights of the clouds; I will make myself like the
>
> Most High." But you are brought down to Sheol, to the far reaches of the
>
> pit. (Isaiah 14:12-15)

Peter Kreeft (1995) refers to Lucifer as, 'the Light-bearer'—the greatest of all creatures, highest angel, Top Guy next to God—and he rebelled and invented evil—many of the angels rebelling with him.

> Their war was a real war. It is not symbolic language. It was not a physical war, because angels don't have physical bodies, but it was a real war, a war of wills, of minds, like a war between paralysed telepaths. The military symbols we use for it are not too strong but too weak....The war was more passionate, intense, and terrifying than any physical war or any physical symbol can convey. (Kreeft, 118)

Fallen Angels have continued not only to oppose God and to denigrate his character but to war against God . The apostle John refers to the arch-angel Lucifer (Satan) as a 'murderer' and 'the father of lies' (John 8:44)
John G. Stackhouse (1998) points out that Judaism and Christianity teach explicitly that a variety of angels (led by the archangel) conspire against the rule of God—and the 'good' of the world:

> Islam speaks of the *jinn*, some of whom are evil and serve Satan, or *iblis*.
> As in Judaism and Christianity these powerful and malignant creatures

once were good....Jews and Christians see the evil beings as 'fallen angels', or former spiritual servants of God. These angels or demons, rebelled against God's sovereignty at some point in the remote past and have since been engaged in an unrelenting campaign to frustrate, if not' destroy, God's work of blessing the world. (Stackhouse 1998, 38,39)

7.2 Rationale for The Fall

Given Anselm's rationale for the fall of angels it would appear that their happiness would have been conterminous with their status; therefore it is likely that their unhappiness would have precipitated their fall from grace. Williams reports Anselm's logic, which is that, "...the rebel angels chose to abandon justice in an attempt to gain happiness for themselves, whereas the good angels chose to persevere in justice even if it meant less happiness." (T. Williams 2013, 4.2) Ergo the happiness of the unholy angels was more important to them than any cause of an omnipotent and benevolent God, such as God's will for humans and for the rest of creation. Regarding the angelic rebellion Peter Vardy (1992) suggests that, "What the Fall does express, however, is the conviction that God created only good and this good then fell from its perfect state in rebellion against God. Indeed later writers (starting with Origen and later Aquinas) were to see the chief feature of Satan and the Devils as being pride. 'They refused to submit to God, they wished to be autonomous...'" (Vardy, 175) We agree with Vardy: that God creates that which is good, and that 'the presence of God' would not be an environment in which rebellion of any sort should take place. Pride would be a good enough reason for a refusal to love and serve God. According to the Oxford dictionary pride can be described as 'the quality of having an excessively high opinion of oneself or one's importance.'

God, Evolution, and Evil's Mystery
Julian Fernandes

Regarding the *'catastrophe of the angel rebellion'* Greg Boyd makes the following assertion, "The greater an angel's potential to soar, the greater its potential to fall: *corruptio optimi pessima*." (2001, 171). However, the rebellion of the angels is not indicative of some kind of 'battle of the titans' but rather, it is indicative of God's concern to allow authentic freedom to creatures—freedom that may have allowed for undesired states of affairs. It is most likely that these creatures were capable of behaving with a freedom that far surpasses that of 'natural man'[61] and that this will have allowed angels the self-determination to contend for autonomy—a drive to achieve absolute self-sufficiency/self-supremacy. Isaiah describes the 'heart' of the matter:

> You said in your heart: 'I will ascend to heaven; above the stars of God. I will sit on the mount of assembly in the far reaches of the north; I will ascend above the heights of the clouds, I will make myself like the Most High" (Isaiah 14:13–14).

Viktor Frankl's (1988) [62] comparison of 'Freedom' and 'Responsibility' speaks volumes:

> Freedom, however, is not the last word. Freedom is only part of the story and half of the truth. Freedom is but the negative aspect of the whole phenomenon whose positive aspect is responsibleness.

---

[61] By 'natural man' we are referring to the state of our species that would have allowed them but one choice in the Garden (Genesis 3)—that of desiring some kind of self-satisfaction, i.e. that they desired the fruit without comprehending the consequences—preferring this option to that of partaking of the tree of life (Genesis 3:24).

[62] Dr Frankl (1905-1997) lost all of his family in the concentration camps of Hitler's Germany but held on to the belief that there was a God in spite of all his observations suggesting the contrary.

God, Evolution, and Evil's Mystery
Julian Fernandes

> In fact, freedom is in danger of degenerating into mere arbitrariness
> unless it is lived in terms of responsibleness… (Frankl 1988)

As has been stated elsewhere, the existence of angelic creatures (including the fallen variety) need not be contentious. Scripture gives abundant significance to their existence. In spite of there being no account of their actual creation in Scripture angels are described as 'created beings' (Revelation 4:11)—they are not gods. As has been suggested above, the creation of these creatures —including the archangel known as Lucifer (Satan)—does not need to bear any relation to the evolutionary process whatsoever. However, there would, in the long term, be consequences for these particular agents (2 Peter 3:5-13; Jude 12-16).[63]

Though Satan's presence in heaven is referred to in Scripture (Job 1:6, 2:1; Revelation 12:7-9), these examples of Satan's presence (whether literal or literary) are 'past-tense' events. It is not necessarily the case, that Satan still occupies the exact same place of authority to which he was initially appointed—though Satan,

---

[63] D.E. Johnson (2001, 164) suggests that the war in heaven that the apostle John sees in symbol was fought, when Jesus suffered and died on the cross outside of Jerusalem and cites Revelation 12:7-9. Johnson's opinion regarding the 'actual' time of the above event is interesting but not significant—in terms of the space-time outworking of God's plan for the creation… However, it is an interesting possibility and it does resonate with the actual declaration of Christ when he declared: 'It is finished' (*consummatum est*) (John 19:30) These were not the words of one acquiescing to his fate but the words of the victorious Son of God who had defeated the works of Satan and had rescued the creation that groans. The crucifixion was the ultimate sacrifice—the resurrection the herald of Creation's release from its bondage to decay and corruption; but, for the fallen variety there became 'new'—hitherto unexperienced constraints—constraints that would eventually see their demise—the eclipse of evil and the realisation of the eschaton.

along with the other fallen angels continues to exercise/abuse certain of the prerogatives of power that were given by God from the onset of their creation[64].

As counterintuitive as the existence of such creatures may seem, particularly regarding the evolutionary process, it is the case that the existence of (angelic) extra-terrestrial life is supported by Scripture and may therefore form part of a biblically-based theodicy. N.T. Wright (2006) reminds us that when C.S. Lewis wrote the *Screw Tape Letters*, Lewis referred to the equal and opposite errors into which people could fall when thinking about the devil; they might take the idea of such a being or concept too seriously—imagining, "...the satan as a being equal and opposite to God or to Jesus..." or, conversely, they might ridicule the very idea of the existence of such entities.

> The satan, as portrayed in scripture and as experienced and taught about by many spiritual guides, is flatly opposed to God, supremely to God incarnate in the crucified and risen Jesus Christ. The claim made by the satan in Matthew 28:18, that to *him* has now been given all authority in heaven and earth. (N. Wright 2006, 71)

---

[64] According to Frederick Tatford (1970, 80) Satan is still numbered among 'the sons of God' and until this privilege is (finally) taken from him in 'the future' Satan still has access into the presence of God. We're not sure how anyone could 'affirm' that the fallen angels are, somehow, as Tatford puts it, 'still numbered among the sons of God'. Fallen angels are, we suggest, though—post the incarnation—constrained to the confines of the known universe and possibly susceptible to the effects of its physical laws. Scripture is clear as to their demise as they shall either cease to exist or be cast out in 'darkness' (Jude 12,13).Wherever they may or may not have their existence it will, we can assume, not be in the New Heavens or Earth — dwelling in the very presence of God.

Wright holds the view that it is quite wrong to think of 'the satan' as 'personal'—in the same way that God and Christ are personal but rather that, 'the satan is sub-personal'. However, Wright does not suggest that the satan is a 'vague or nebulous force—quite the reverse' (**N. Wright, 71**) We, however, fail to see the problem—and prefer to consider Satan as (very) personal—so personal in fact that this creature is desirous of the elimination of the 'vessel made of clay' (Jeremiah 18:4 & Romans 9:21). Moreover, a 'vague or nebulous' concept could not, conceivably, have 'personal' objectives.

7.3 Biospheric Consequences:

The question arises as to how the [continued] rebellion of such creatures actually affects the physical realm. How does it manifest itself?

Though not specifically addressing the influence of incorporeal agents, Marilyn McCord Adams (1999) suggests that, when evil (unspecified origin) threatens we can take measures by assessing the risk factors, "...be it by taking care not to drop matches in dry forests, by boarding up windows against hurricanes, by sending peace-keeping forces...by working long hours in scientific laboratories to discover cures for crippling diseases..." (Adams-McCord 1999, 181) McCord Adams is not suggesting that the above are inherently evil (though the effects of war produces untold suffering) but that there needs to be an awareness that these eventualities may bring about harms. These harms—often considered as 'natural evil' are harms that may, though, be brought about by the influence or unseen actions of extra-terrestrials—fallen angels. To suggest that such 'august' creatures as angels can have no influence on the physical world would be to deny Scripture. Moreover, these creatures, though incorporeal, are able—as is the creator God—to affect change to the physical order.

God, Evolution, and Evil's Mystery

Julian Fernandes

To suggest that fallen angels do not have the ability to bring about: forest fires, hurricanes, war and disease would be to ignore what Scripture affirms—that the immaterial can bring about changes to the 'material'. If this were not so then Scripture would not be replete with examples of how it does exactly that. Moreover, it is the case that the Creator God, though incorporeal, is able to influence/persuade the creation into being. Referring to Quantum Theory Richard Swinburne (1998) makes that point that Quantum theory indicates the most fundamental laws of nature, "...the laws governing the behaviour of very small-scale particles, are probabilistic, i.e. indeterministic; but that, in general, small-scale indeterminacies cancel out on the large scale, leading to virtually deterministic behaviour of the medium size objects with which we interact— tables and chairs, trees and persons." (Swinburne 1998, 116) It is not that ways have to be found to justify the unseen interaction between the 'material' and the 'immaterial' but that modern advances in theoretical physics have brought to light ideas that had been considered most unlikely.

John Hick (2010) refers to, "the idea of a fall of angelic beings preceding and accounting for both the fall of man and the disordered and dysteleological features of the natural world." (331) He admits that such a speculation has its attractions but views it with some disdain—comparing it with that of the 'old Greek pantheon'. Hick adds, that the above idea was, in the first century, "... a contemporary Jewish understanding of disease which seems also to have been shared by Jesus himself." (332). Hick's concern here seems to be that such an idea would be a denial of creation's 'natural goodness'. In contradistinction to Hick's view, the argument here is that the intrusion of angels into the material world does not deny the existence of an evolutionary pathway; neither does such an intrusion militate against the notion of a 'good' creation. However, our understanding of 'good' is not that the creation was ever 'perfectly morally good', so it has to mean something else. Stephen T. Davis' view is that, "God judged his creation to be very good in that it was a harmonious, beautiful, smoothly working cosmos rather than an ugly, churning chaos over which the Holy Spirit had moved (Genesis. 1:2)." (S. Davis 2001, 73) The Creation was as God intended.

R. J. Russell (**2008**) points out that, "the Second Law of Thermodynamics provides an example at the level of physics of what is needed if the consequences of sinful acts are to be expressed physically, including dissipation and disruption, as well as the consequences of virtuous acts of beauty and goodness." (**258**) This potentially, we maintain, would had been allowed for prior to the genesis of creation. If the Second Law is the necessary component—the one constant that produces the bountiful array of life that emanates through the biological processes as well as producing the entropic consequences that bring about predation, parasitism, plague and even 'natural disasters'—then its inclusion would have been either an intentional act of the Creator of the universe or otherwise. We advocate the former, i.e. that it was both a necessary and intentional act—taken by God before the creation of the physical universe.

In Genesis 2:17 the author refers not only to the tree of life but also to the 'tree of the knowledge of good and evil'[65]. The linguistic use of the term 'good and evil' in Scripture is defined as an actual state or potentiality. In other words 'good and evil' had prior linguistic and experiential reality with regards to the actions of created agents.

---

[65] C. John Collins (2011, 65) refers to the symbolic references (e.g. Proverbs 3:18;11:30;13:12;15:4) and suggests that the use of such language warrants us in finding the this tree to be some kind 'sacrament' that (somehow) sustains or confirms someone in his moral condition—this being the reason for God's banishment of the couple from 'the garden'.

For any such 'actions' to have real effects there needs to be the 'physical' potential, i.e. the potentiality for incorporeal agents to bring about less than positive outcomes within the biosphere: to interfere with the creation.

7.4 Post Fall Subjugation

God's necessary plans and intentionality are not to be confused with Paul's words in Romans 8:20-21 where the apostle states that, "...the creation was [subjected][66] to futility, not willingly, but because of him who subjected it, in hope that the creation itself will be set free from its bondage to corruption and obtain the freedom of the glory of the children of God." In this passage, as elsewhere in the letter (Hendriksen 1980), Paul is referring to a 'post Adamic Fall' subjugation and not to any plans or actions taken by the creator before the creation of the physical universe. *NB: It was God who (post Adamic fall) subjected the creation— not: angels, demons or mankind.* The subjugation that the apostle refers to, moreover, is not related to the creation of the universe but, specifically, to the Adamic Fall as recorded in Genesis 3. Leon Morris states that Scripture never assigns (either to 'Adam' or 'Satan') the power to bring about such far-reaching change, and that there is no reason to think of Adam or of Satan acting in hope for the future. "...hope is characteristic of God, who may indeed be called 'the God of hope' (Romans 15:13) The Adamic fall is not the last word; the last word is with hope." (Morris 1988, 321-322) When would this subjugation of nature have taken place? We suggest that, as far as Paul was concerned, it would have been after the event in the garden (Genesis 3:15); here the writer specifically refers to the condemnation of the 'serpent'. Paul, most likely, would not have presumed that God had pre-ordained the present (created) evolutionary biosphere in order to deal with the rebellion of either 'Adam' or angels.

---

[66] Greek *Hupotassō* meaning to rank under—denoting subjugation. (Vine, 1109)

God, Evolution, and Evil's Mystery
Julian Fernandes

John Bimson (2006) refers to the work of Andrew Linzey (2000) who suggests that Paul's use of 'bondage to decay' refers to 'predation and parasitism—all the apparent violence and cruelty inherent in the structures of nature'. Regarding Paul's reference to Genesis 3 James Dunn (2003, 96-97) suggests that the allusion is clear—and that the theme is familiar. Dunn states that the apostle draws the obvious implication from the function of the tree of life in Genesis 2-3, that death was not a part of the original divine *intention* in creation. However, despite some ambiguity, Dunn offers what he thinks Paul might be saying:

> What Paul seems to be saying is something like this: (1) All humanity shares a common subserviency to sin and death. This is not merely a natural fleshness, a created mortality. Sin is bound up with it, a falling short of God's intended best. Death is the outcome of a breakdown within creation. (2) there is a two-sidedness to this state of affairs, involving both sin as an accountable action of individual responsibility…(3)…this state is the consequence of humanity's refusal to acknowledge God, of the creature's attempt to dispense with the creator. When humankind declared its independence from God, it abandoned the only power which can overcome the sin which uses the weakness of the flesh, the only power which can overcome death… (Dunn 2003, 97)

Dunn's summary offers a reasonable account of the 'life potential' offered to the imago Dei—in contradistinction to mankind's adherence to acquiesce to another's choice—that of Satan. Indeed, Genesis 3:22 informs us that the man had not eaten of the tree of life, 3:24, and that there were cherubim guarding the way to *the tree of life* so that they could not partake of its fruit.

God, Evolution, and Evil's Mystery
Julian Fernandes

The occupants of the garden had 'eaten' from the tree of the knowledge of good and evil (Genesis 3:6). This was not at all surprising as the quest for knowledge is empowering. It would have been, we suggest, the quest for knowledge, independent of God, where the problem lay—the quest for power and personal sovereignty—perhaps the same quest sought by Satan and the fallen angels. God had made provision for the sustaining of the life of the first Adam .The tree of life had not, previously, been out of bounds. Physical death was however the 'order'. Without the direct intervention of the source of life (God the creator) it was the necessary consequence of one of the fundamental laws of physics: the second law of thermodynamics—what William R. Stoeger (2007) describes as, "...the underlying physical reason for the transience and fragility of any physically or chemically based system—any material entity..." (96).

Death was natural yet the possibility of eternal (physical) life seemed to be 'on offer'. If eternal (physical) existence was possible, why should God have included such a defining set of rules? There are two reasons that we wish to consider as 'reasons' for God's inclusion of the Second Law within the laws that govern physical reality:

1. That, in order to produce 'conscious physicality' in carbon-based creatures, the process of biological evolution was the only way God could have brought about his ultimate (good) objectives—the production of all 'creaturely value'—ultimately the Imago Dei.
2. To dispose of the 'present problem of evil'—the problem that had manifested itself within the physical cosmology—that is the present universe. Moreover, we maintain that it is within the physical/material reality that evil

presently pervades and that it will not obtain at the eschaton as God _will have_ completely eradicated it.

Belief in the sovereignty and integrity of God leads us to the conclusion that God is working his purposes out and that belief in God's benevolence can be upheld. However, the world 'has been', 'is being' and 'will be' subjected to degradation of all kinds until the eschaton. Scripture tells us (Ps. 24:1-2) that this world and all that is in it belongs to God and _yet_ Scripture also states that, 'the whole world lies in the power of the evil one.' (1 Jn. 5:19) and that, '...an enemy has brought corruption to the earth...' (Matt. 13:28). There is, we maintain, no contradiction here as 'ownership' or 'authorship' does not preclude either intrusion or the out-workings of the decisions of 'minds' other than God's. Gregory Boyd argues that, "If the cosmos is not something of a democracy[67], it has to be something of a tyrannical monarchy." (1997, 118-119) We do not hold that the cosmos is anything like a democracy neither do we believe that 'sovereignty' necessitates tyrannical monarchy—at least not where the God of the Bible is concerned—'gods' are another matter. What is clear from both observation and from Scripture is that the earth is not anything like 'heaven' but that it is a place full of all that might be expected if an enemy of God 'wished to' usurp God's authority and to tarnish God's reputation. This 'present' state—as recorded in Scripture and as observed by the discerning eye—is not an example of chaos ruling over sovereignty or any other kind of alleged (dualistic) cosmic conflict. It is not at all what it seems; it is, in spite of what seems to be 'evidence' to the contrary, "God's future, and this is more than the future time. It is the future of time itself—time past, time present,

---

[67] Whilst not sharing all of Boyd's particular views of the openness of God we appreciate his sentiments here, i.e. that there has to be activity in the creation that is not under the control of a cosmic puppeteer; this applies to the actions (causes and effects) of both humans and angels.

and time to come. In his future, God comes to his creation and through the power of his righteousness and justice, frees it for his kingdom, and makes it the dwelling place of his glory." (Bauckham 1999)

Summary:

1. Considering the pre-existence of Angels it can be concluded that, though created by God, they were not created along with the rest of the creative order within the evolutionary system. In other words, they were created outside of the known space/time continuum.

2. The event that precipitated the rebellion of some of these angelic agents would have been 'known' by God prior to the 'beginnings' of the universe. Ergo, this would have been a major factor regarding God's planned intentions for the material universe.

God, Evolution, and Evil's Mystery
Julian Fernandes

Part 8. That only such a world as this could make possible the incarnation of the divine Son and thereby the defeat of the angels and the implantation of justice through the power of the Cross:

8.1 Only such a world

Simon Conway Morris (2003) refers to the significance of the evolution of humans, or something very closely related. He states that, "We may be unique, but paradoxically those properties that define our uniqueness can still be inherent in the evolutionary process. In other words, if we humans had not evolved then something more or less identical would have emerged sooner or later." (2003, 198) Whatever the actuality of the evolutionary process mankind's place in the evolutionary scale of events has been inevitable and is exceptional within the created order. Evolution was given, seemingly, a clear direction—there was, what may be considered a 'blueprint' for the process. William Carroll (quoting various sources) succinctly outlines the theistic implications within the biological process:

> Although chance events are frequent and important in biological evolution, rendering its actual course indeterminate or unpredictable in exact outcome from any particular stage, these events and their short and long-term effects—whether they be of point mutations at the level of molecular DNA, or the impact of a meteorite—are always within a context of regularities, constraints, and possibilities. Thus, to refer to such events as 'pure chance' or to assert blithely that evolution proceeds by purely

chance events is much less than a precise description of this source of unpredictability in biological evolution... Furthermore, even though the contemporary natural sciences often seek to discover efficient causes without reference to purposes (final causes), any ordering of efficient causes and their effects implicitly acknowledges and presupposes that the efficient causes and the processes which embody them are directed towards the realization of certain specific types of ends. Efficient causes always have certain specifiable **effects**. (Carroll 2000)

The point being made here is that an omnipotent God can bring order out of chaos or order out of what may appear to be undirected evolutionary processes. However one discerns the means through which the God of the Judeo/Christian Scriptures 'directs' creative processes, Earth is the 'blue sphere' that God had prepared for the arrival of homo sapiens[68] and for such an event as the incarnation of Christ and the annunciation of 'release for the captives'(Isaiah 42:7). As has been previously argued this world is the only possible world, in which there could have arisen intelligent carbon-based life forms. Indeed, as Michael Murray (2008) points out, we have no knowledge of any other such worlds in which biological evolution as we know it could succeed.

Regarding the creation of this world the Genesis text states: "God saw everything he had made and it was very good". (1:31). God sustains the world as well as the

---

[68] William Stone (2014, 53-81) suggests that Adam could be placed at the route of the Homo *erectus/ergaster* to Homo sapiens lineage around 1.8 million years ago. Stone qualifies this by adding (p80) that his conclusion was somewhat contingent on the acceptance of a number of presuppositions that were "bound up with current paleoanthropological models." Stone commented that he had not addressed the wider issues of relating the *'human'* fossil record to the biblical narrative, which is something of particular importance.

universe within the boundaries[69] He has set for it. According to the Genesis text, the creative results were not only good but they were 'very good'; 'everything had gone to plan'; the result being that it was '<u>very good</u>'. There followed, what *appeared to be*, a 'dark side' to the process[70]—that of the negative side of the Second Law of Thermodynamics—the increase of entropy that ensured the likelihood of the evolutionary process. However, what may appear to some observers to be the dark side of the laws of physics need be nothing of the sort. Rather, the laws, as ordained by the creator, were a necessary ingredient for the creation and development of carbon-based life—culminating in the 'late' arrival of the image bearers of God. It is by the laws of physics that the triune God is able to bring about ultimate justice; God, in Christ, is able to give of himself on the cross so that there could be resolution and reconciliation[71].

---

[69] What is meant by 'boundaries' is the limits that God may have preordained for the development of his creation both cosmological [in terms of the expansion of the universe] and biological [in terms of God's restrictions on the limits of evolutionary development as well as God's prohibitions on any undesired interference to that development—by any created beings—humans or otherwise.]

[70] "..the Second Law taken in isolation leads us to predict a future which is one of disorder and ultimate decay..." (Hough 2010, 143)

[71] With reference to the efficacy of the Cross of Christ the apostle Paul states that, "...while we were enemies we were reconciled to God by the death of his Son, much more, now that we are reconciled, shall we be saved by his life. More than that, we also rejoice in God through our Lord Jesus Christ, through whom we have now received reconciliation." (Romans 5:10) .Christ has dealt with the problem of evil through his death on the cross. The cross is the ultimate act of justice through which God deals with the sin of the world. Paul states that , "...if righteousness were through the law, then Christ died for no purpose." (Galatians 2:21) The acceptance of God's offer of unconditional forgiveness is a matter of grace but it is also a matter of the heart as is made clear in Romans 10:9: "If you confess with your mouth that Jesus is Lord and believe in your heart that God raised him from the dead, you will be saved.". However it is that reconciliation and grace

God, Evolution, and Evil's Mystery
Julian Fernandes

The argument in this thesis is that any kinds of harms—whether the results of predation, parasitism and plague or the consequence of plate tectonic movement etc.—should be regarded as consequences of, mostly, a necessary-natural-state-of-affairs. However, the 'evil' that does manifest itself within the world is far from natural, rather it is the result of deviancy within the minds and wills of both terrestrial and extra-terrestrial beings—ergo it is 'moral' rather than natural, and it manifests itself in every hideous shape and form.

It is this 'angelic moral deviancy' and resultant rebellion that the Creator God had to consider prior to the initiation of the creation ex nihilo; 'omniscience' would have been key to the knowledge required by God to outmanoeuvre the powerful enemies of God. Our argument here is that it was the mind of God alone that contained the wherewithal to bring about a biosphere that, on the surface, would have appeared random yet beneath the veneer of chance and necessity there lay a deeper reality over time—an unfurling of the telos of God. Perhaps it was the 'unfurling' of God's plans for creation that enabled/allowed the angels' insight into the (perceived) plans and purposes of God. Whatever the truth, the fallen angels could not have understood the actual plans of God— plans that were to bring about the redemption of a cosmos tainted by the actions and interventions of deviants. It was the incarnation—the death— the resurrection into 'new life' of the second person of the Trinity that they would have been ignorant of—for if they had not been ignorant of God's plans and intentions, they would not have allowed such a state of affairs to obtain—for it was to, eventually, bring about their demise.

---

work together, the important point is that this momentous act of sacrifice and of reconciliation is, according to Scripture, found in Christ alone (Acts 4:12).

8.2 The Goal of Creation

Scripture attests to the incarnational objectives of the second person of the Trinity. Andrew and Trotter (1997) refer to the importance of eschatology as recorded in the letter to the Hebrews—pointing out that the prologue catalogues what had happened in Christ, "... in a historical progression of events moving from his role as Creator to Redeemer to heavenly intermediary for his people." (208).

> ...to which of the angels has he (God) ever said, 'Sit at my right hand until I make your enemies a footstool for your feet.'(Christ) ...for a little while made a little lower than the angels.....crowned with glory and honour because of the suffering of death, so that by the grace of God he might taste death for everyone...that through death he might destroy the one who has the power of death, that is, the devil. (Hebrews 1:13; 2:7,14).

The irony is that God, by allowing for the physical laws that bring about what may be considered the worst possible state of affairs, actually allows for the best possible state of affairs to obtain—victory over sin and death. Colin Dye (2013) refers to Genesis 3:15 as being the first glimpse of the gospel, the first foreshadowing of the cross, and it points specifically to the victory of God:

> This first prediction of triumph identified the woman's seed, or offspring, as the one who would be completely victorious. It was later revealed to the prophets that this 'seed' would be the Messiah, the Christos or 'Anointed Man', who would establish God's righteous rule and eradicate evil." (Dye 2013)

God, Evolution, and Evil's Mystery
Julian Fernandes

Regarding the incarnation Adrio König (1989) points out that when the apostle Paul states that 'all things are created for Christ' (Colossians 1:16), "...here we have the goal of creation. Creation is aimed toward Christ as its target; it moves toward him, and in him it will reach its goal.[72]" (1989, 26)

Ivor Davidson refers to God's 'end designs' when he says that, "The God who saves is the God who is creator, sustainer, redeemer and perfecter of all things, the one who elects to enter into irrevocable union with materiality, whose Spirit animates all life, and who surely has purposes for all that he has made. While there is much that we cannot say about the details of what this entails eschatologically, God, it seems, intends that not just humans but creatures of all kinds should attain the glory of freedom and fulfilment in relation to their creator." (2011, 11)

Jonathan R. Wilson (2013) states that it is when Christians progress a Trinitarian doctrine of creation (in what Wilson refers to as "being in dialectic with redemption") it is 'then' that they have good news for their interlocutors—indeed for society: "Given our convictions about creation...we may know that the refusal to believe in Christ as the telos of the universe will lead to despair even as society develops strategies, practices and products to ameliorate deny and manage the despair." (Wilson 2013, 20-29)

> He is the image of the invisible God, the firstborn of all creation. For
> by him all things were created, in heaven and on earth, visible and

---

[72] König points out that there is no contradiction between this and such statements as Romans 11:36 and Hebrews 2:10 where it we read that God (the Father) is the purpose of creation—for there is no disunity between Father and Son. The same applies to Hebrews 2:10 and also to Colossians 1:16.

invisible, whether thrones or dominions or rulers or authorities—all things were created through him and for him. And he is before all things, and in him all things hold together. And he is the head of the body, the church. He is the beginning, the firstborn from the dead, that in everything he might be preeminent. For in him all the fullness of God was pleased to dwell, and through him to reconcile to himself all things, whether on earth or in heaven, making peace by the blood of his cross. (Colossians 1:15-20)

N.T.Wright (2003) refers to the above passage from Paul's letter to the Colossians as, "...a spectacular early Christian poem [which] places Jesus' resurrection (1:18) in parallel with the creation of the world (1:15), seeing it as the ground and origin of what the creator has now accomplished and is now implementing, namely the reconciliation of all things to him." (239) Wright's conviction, that the very shape of the poem insists that Jesus' resurrection, as a one-off event, is an act not of the elimination of the original creation but of its fulfilment (239), fits in with our argument. Moreover, Wright's conclusion that, "...the one through whom all things were made in the first place, the one through whom all things cohere, the one in and through all things are now brought into a new relationship with the creator God and with one another.." coheres with the argument here—that, the eternal Son of God—through his life, death and resurrection reconciled all things to himself—" He [God] disarmed the rulers and authorities and put them to open shame, by triumphing over them in him [Christ]." (Colossians 2:15)

8.3 The Justice of God

God, Evolution, and Evil's Mystery
Julian Fernandes

Without penalty any notion of law is meaningless. Any action by agents with the capacity to will to choose brings with it the consequences of that action. Peter Lowman (2002) says, "… to the biblical worldview, the world as a whole was condemned to purposelessness by the first humans' assertion of independence from God that we call the Fall. The results were meaninglessness—futility." (53) This 'one act of rebellion' (as reported in Genesis 3) was, de facto, the precursor to both condemnation and intervention—God's intervention being particularly delineated in Genesis 2 and 3 where the text refers to: 'a loss of life potential' (2:17); 'increased pain awareness' (3:16); 'a radical change in the environs' (3:17-19), and the loss of access to the 'tree', which is, in some way analogous of '*the source of the sustenance of life*' (3:23,24) . But, this 'one' act of rebellion by the 'Adamic' pair was not the source of the Problem of Evil, it was rather the outworking of the rebellion of angels that had taken place 'prior' to the creation of the physical universe[73]. But it was within this physical universe (within the constraints allowed by the physical laws that God had ordained) that the effects of these laws (outside of the garden) had already been made manifest. It was to the outside of this 'Eden'—'sacred place' (Walton 2009, 82)—that the first pair would have been expelled. As with the angels who were cast out of heaven, so the man and woman were cast out of Eden not because they had the will to choose but that they chose to oppose God—to abjure from loving and serving and enjoying the presence of their creator God. Both the 'casting out' of the Adamic pair (Genesis 3:22,23) and the casting down of Satan and his angels (Revelation 12:7-12; Luke 10:18) entailed banishment and exile—Imago Dei from

---

[73] 'Events' *prior to the beginning of the space/time continuum* are not events that can be measured as such; however, the need for intelligible communication dictates the use of time words and of tenses; consequently, when we refer to an authentic occurrence before the creation of the Universe we have little option but to use such language.

the paradise—from the potential for life in all its fullness ; the angels from the presence of God—into an environment from which there would be no exit (Jude 13; Revelation 20). [74]

8.4 Beyond Shadowlands

It stands to reason that if God were 'able' (due to God's omnipotence) to create a world without the deleterious effects of entropy, then it is reasonable to ask why it is God may not have taken this direction when working out his grand plan for the creation of the universe. Could God have not produced a better environment than planet earth so that there was less likelihood of—at least natural disasters? The answer is, unequivocally in the negative; and it is for this reason: This universal system is not merely the best of all possible systems conducive to the formation of biological life—life in all its vulnerability.It is more crucially, the only system that would have allowed for God to deal with the 'Universal' Problem of Evil: to prepare a biological pathway for the arrival of mankind—and therefor the possibility of the incarnation of the second person of the Trinity, and henceforth the redemption of creation through the Cross of Christ, so that the redeemed creation could dwell with the Godhead on the new earth.

That the ascension of Christ is significant is beyond doubt. However, what may not be so readily observable (unless seen through the lens of theoretical physics —into the 'world' of parallel universes) is the possibility that the new world order

---

[74] Could it be the case that these creatures, having been cast out of heaven, infecting both the biosphere and their own self[s]—were, as fallen angels, lesser creatures with diminished powers —in some way subject to the laws of physics? We can but speculate. They, however, have continued to war against the creation that God had declared good.

God, Evolution, and Evil's Mystery
Julian Fernandes

(new heavens and new earth) may already exist—having been developing in tandem with the known world—that this is possibly where Christ dwells at present—is somehow synonymous with that which will appear from 'heaven'—as the vision of John records: "And I saw the holy city, new Jerusalem, coming down out of heaven from God, prepared as a bride adorned for her husband." (Revelation 21:2)

J.J. Wilson describes the 'new heavens and new earth' as, "...not a second creation or a simple restoration of the first heaven and earth; it is the redemption of creation for its telos [that] takes place in Jesus Christ. The blessedness of the 'beatitudes' is now fulfilled in the new creation." (2013, 136)

C. S. Lewis said that Christianity does not teach us to desire 'a total release'—as if we were to be emancipated from the physical: "We desire, like St Paul, not to be un-clothed but to be re-clothed; to find not the formless Everywhere-and-Nowhere but the promised land, that Nature which will be always and perfectly–as presently Nature is partially and intermittently–the instrument for that music which will then arise between Christ and us." (1998, 171,172) Moreover, Lewis considers that entering heaven is to become more human than ever possible on this planet. In one of his 'children's stories Lewis paints a picture of a bleak world in which there is no summer only winter. The 'coming world' may be the world beyond our present experience but Scripture assures us that life in this, as yet unknown world, is beyond the tainted reach of 'Shadowlands'. It can be further supposed that the paradise of God may somehow co-exist with the known cosmos. In other words, The evolution of the best of all possible worlds (in which

God, Evolution, and Evil's Mystery

Julian Fernandes

entropy has no effects[75]) may have been being created at the same 'time' as this (the best of all possible worlds in which the problem of evil is dealt a fatal blow). The possibility of such a parallel new world order is not, considering the nature and character of the God of Scripture, an unreasonable or implausible assumption. Moreover, it is not a less reasonable projection than the novel ideas regarding the happenstance of parallel universes.

We are of the firm opinion that it is because of the inexhaustible benevolence of God that the 'old order' has been allowed to continue thus far. Moreover, it is because of the gracious mercy of God that every possible opportunity is given for mankind to respond to 'kindness of God' as the apostle Paul refers to in his letter to the Romans. (2:4)

As much as it is possible to offer a theodicy or defence; it is quite another thing to satisfy all the challenges proffered against the possibility of, not only the existence of the God of the Bible, but of this same God's goodness. In the Eight-Step argument offered here we have, what is, as close to an evolutionary theodicy as is possible. There is, however, one area of thought that we need to consider—that of 'Free-Will'. The notion of free-will may be considered a flaw in the argument because, it might be argued that God will have taken a step too far in that any cause and effect from free-will choices would be, ultimately, God's

---

[75] Projecting forward to the actualization of the Grace of God in a 'new world order', R.J. Russell states insightfully that, "in its most simple form it might mean that the New Creation will not include thermodynamics since it contributes to natural evil. In a slightly more complex form it might mean that the New Creation *will* not include thermodynamics to the extent that it produces natural evils, though it might include it to the extent that it produces natural goods." (Russell 2008).

responsibility. In response to this sentiment, we would argue that the free-will expressed in both angelic and human actions were, for the Creator, a price worth paying—and for the creation—a glorious expression of ontological creative genius. The alternative is not a consideration—indeed there would be no need of any notion of defence should free-will be either an illusion or a state of affairs that is beyond the creative ability of an omnipotent God.

Let the reader decide which of the two would have produced a better state of affairs: a sterile, mechanistic world void of personality and free-will, in which there existed only the pretence of personality or a world in which God's personality is reflected in the Imago Dei—the fallen and the redeemed?

Conclusion

Throughout the duration of this research project we have sought to establish whether or not it was possible to successfully argue that the God of biblical theism—being identified as the master craftsman of the creation of the physical universe—could possibly be the architect, creator/ sustainer of life throughout the [evolutionary] history of the biosphere—and have concluded that it is entirely plausible to conclude that the God of Christian Scriptures,who is both omnipotent and benevolent, ordained the known physical laws so as to bring about the best of possible outcomes.

We reasoned that the creation should be considered 'good' as opposed to 'perfect'—and that there is sufficient reason to refute the notion of the creation being perfect at its inception and therefore—as the result of either an Angelic or Adamic Fall—that creation suffered a catastrophic failure to the extent that there was a change to the physical laws through which predation, parasitism, plague and death entered the experience of all carbon-based life forms.

We have, furthermore, argued that in spite of the difficulty in advocating God's goodness within an evolutionary framework the implications do not present an insurmountable hurdle to the work of evolutionary theodicy—as argued in part two of this thesis.

We considered the ingenuity of philosophical theologians—in their attempt to offer an alternative for the God of Scripture, and argued that though their efforts are creative—at least in terms of an alternative view of the deity—they are not relevant to any defence that takes the traditional views of God's character seriously. Moreover, we reasoned that the 'Ground of Being' alternative, and that of process theology, and other philosophical theologians are not at all convincing—and are an unnecessary deviancy from the traditional view God as a [Triune] personality: 'A Determinate Entity'.

We interacted with various defences/theodicies, that in the light of biological evolution, have offered differing perspectives—ranging from, what appears to be an obscure scenario involving retrospective Kairological—post 'Adamic Fall' judgement—to an up-to-date review of the theodicies of Irenaeus and Augustine. It was throughout our lengthy interaction with all of these defences/theodicies that the eight-part argument was devised and developed.

In the second part of the thesis we introduced and discussed an 'Eight Step Defence' (we refer to it as a defence rather than a theodicy). In this eight-step-defence we argued that it is good for God to create a world such as this—and that

God, Evolution, and Evil's Mystery
Julian Fernandes

such a world as this could only obtain via an evolutionary process—that it is only such a world as this that is capable of being transformed into the new creation—as it is in this world, at the right time, that mankind 'became' . We made the case for the existence of angels, and for their existence prior to the 'space/tie continuum—that it was a good thing that God had created angels with free-will—even though these fallen angels continued to oppose God's purposes, especially with regards to God's purposes for mankind—both on this earth and on the new earth. We argued that, at a particular juncture in time, the second person of the Trinity became a man so that, in due course, He, and only He, could, through his death and resurrection, defeat the evil brought about by the rebellion of angels—making possible a way back from 'Eden' for mankind—from alienation into the presence of God on the New Earth.

Derek John White

www.ingramcontent.com/pod-product-compliance
Lightning Source LLC
LaVergne TN
LVHW041321200726
843509LV00009B/573